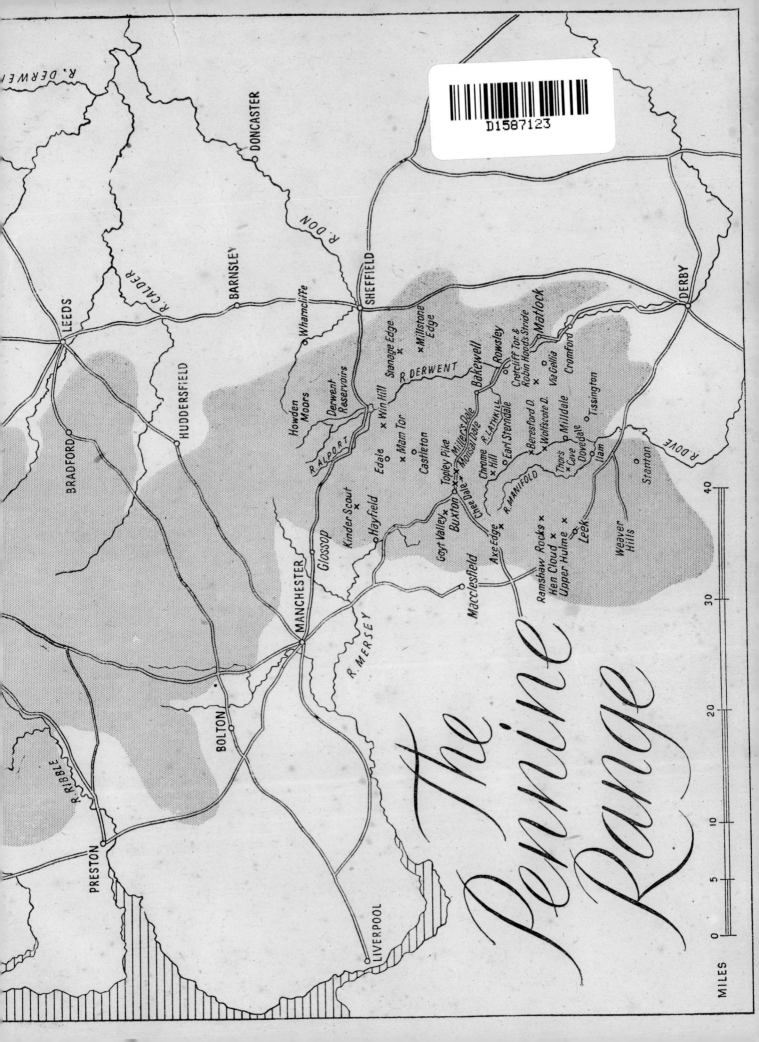

The Pennine Range

MILES
0 5 10 20 30 40

THE BACKBONE OF ENGLAND

By the Same Author

ESCAPE TO THE HILLS
LAKELAND THROUGH THE LENS
SNOWDONIA THROUGH THE LENS
SCOTLAND THROUGH THE LENS
LAKELAND HOLIDAY
SNOWDON HOLIDAY
HIGHLAND HOLIDAY
LAKELAND JOURNEY

MALHAM COVE FROM THE UPPER TERRACE

THE BACKBONE
OF ENGLAND

by

W. A. POUCHER, F.R.P.S.

WITH
PHOTOGRAPHS BY THE
AUTHOR

LONDON: COUNTRY LIFE LIMITED
2-10 TAVISTOCK STREET, COVENT GARDEN, W.C. 2

First Published 1946

The Paper and Binding of this
Book conform to the Authorised
Economy Standards.

Printed in Great Britain by
Billing and Sons Ltd., Guildford and Esher

PREFACE

Lovers of British hill scenery have for years been drawn to the Scottish Highlands, the English Lakes and to North Wales, sometimes through their advertised splendours, but more often by the glowing accounts of their attractions given by devotees to one or other of these districts. No such publicity has formerly been given to the Backbone of England, which is perhaps familiar to those who live on its borders, but is nevertheless comparatively unknown to the vast majority of tourists in the country.

The whole district is covered by a great network of roads, most of which carry good surfaces and are thus suitable for the motorist who wishes to get some idea of its beauties. The Pennines are, however, ideally suited to the walker who desires to enjoy the scenery alone, for here he will find fresh air, healthy exercise, and profound solitude in the high places, all of which may be reached by easy ways that do not involve rock climbing or danger of any sort that is usually associated with remote and inaccessible mountainous country. Moreover, he will find plenty of comfortable inns in which to stay, while the hiker with simpler tastes is adequately provided for by a chain of Youth Hostels giving easy access to all the places of interest.

I spent six weeks exploring this long line of hills, together with their complementary dales, and although I had previously visited some of them, I searched for and discovered on this occasion not only a number of spectacular scenes hidden away in the hills, but also a galaxy of loveliness in the valleys and in the charming villages which are dotted about them. I have portrayed herein all those places which I thought would interest the reader, and in the text have described my experiences and given such details as will enable him to find and enjoy them himself.

Most people on holiday carry a camera, and they will have ample opportunities of practising their art in the Pennines. The photographs in this book could have been taken by anyone with an eye for a picture who was prepared to wait for suitable lighting. I have no secrets, and use a modern miniature camera, panchromatic film, and straightforward development, all of which I have described in great detail in other works devoted to the British Hills.

COURTLANDS,   W. A. POUCHER.
KINGSWOOD,
SURREY.

CONTENTS

(Plates are referred to in italic type)

FRONTISPIECE: MALHAM COVE FROM THE UPPER TERRACE

PREFACE 5

INTRODUCTION 9

THE HILLS 10
Axe Edge 11

THE DALES 12
Askrigg in Wensleydale . . . 12

THE PENNINE WAY 13
Littondale 14
Dufton 15

ILAM AND DISTRICT 16
The Manifold Valley from above Thor's Cave . 17
Ilam 18
Bridge over the Manifold at Ilam . . 19
The Weaver Hills from Stanton . . 20
Tissington 21
Thor's Cave 22
Massive Column supporting the arches of Thor's Cave 23

THE DOVE 26
An enchanting stretch of Dovedale . 24, 25
Dovedale. Castle Rocks . . . 27
Dovedale. Stepping Stones . . . 28
Looking north along Dovedale . . 29
Dove Holes 30
Packhorse Bridge at Milldale . . 31
Lode Mill and Dove Cottage at the entrance to Wolfscote Dale 32
Limestone bastions of Wolfscote Dale . 33
A quiet stretch of the Dove in Wolfscote Dale . 34
The end of Wolfscote Dale . . . 35
The entrance to Beresford Dale . . 36
Pike Pool, Beresford Dale . . . 37

MATLOCK AND DISTRICT 38
A Cottage near Stanton-in-Peak . . 39
Matlock. Riber Castle and High Tor from the Heights of Abraham 40
The Mill in Via Gellia . . . 41

Cromford. Looking to Middleton from the Black Rocks 42
Stone Circle near Robin Hood's Stride . . 43
Robin Hood's Stride 44
Cratcliff Tor. The Owl Gully . . 45

THE LATHKILL TO EARL STERNDALE . . 46
Earl Sterndale. Inn Sign . . . 46
Chrome Hill from Crowdecote . . 47
River Bradford near Haddon Hall . 48
The Lathkill at Alport . . . 49
Over Haddon and the Lathkill from Conksbury Bridge 50
Lathkill Dale at its junction with Cales Dale . 51

THE WYE 52
Waterfall in Monsal Dale . . . 53
Bakewell Bridge 54
Monsal Dale 55
The western end of Chee Dale through which the Wye flows down to Miller's Dale . 56, 57
Mill at the entrance to Miller's Dale . . 58
Miller's Dale 59
Limestone Cliffs in Miller's Dale . . 60
Chee Tor 61
Chee Dale 62
Stepping Stones in Chee Dale . . 63
Topley Pike 64
Great Rocks Dale 65

BUXTON AND DISTRICT 66
Climbers on Hen Cloud . . . 67
Buxton. The River Wye passing through the Gardens 68
Sunlight in the Goyt Valley . . . 69
Ramshaw Rocks 70
The Toad, Ramshaw Rocks . . . 71
Hen Cloud from Upper Hulme . . 72
Hen Cloud 73
The Staffordshire Roaches from Hen Cloud . 74
Hen Cloud 75

STANAGE EDGE TO THE " SURPRISE " . 76
Stanage Edge. High Neb from Jacob's Ladder . 77
High Neb 78
Millstones at Stanage Edge . . . 79
Millstone Edge 80
Win Hill and Bamford Moor from the "Surprise" 81

CONTENTS—*continued*

THE CASTLETON DISTRICT 82
   The Winnats 83
   Lose Hill, Back Tor and Win Hill from Mam Tor 84
   Back Tor 85
   Mam Tor, the " Shivering Mountain " . . 86
   The Hope Valley from Lose Hill . . . 87

EDALE AND KINDER SCOUT . . . 90
   Edale and Kinder Scout from the Great Ridge 88, 89
   Kinder Downfall 91
   The Head of Edale from Ringing Roger . 92
   Crowden Tower from Crowden Brook, Kinder
     Scout 93
   Mud Grough on the summit of Kinder Scout . 94
   Featherbed Moss from the "Boxing Glove" Stones
     on Ashop Edge 95
   Win Hill from Woodlands Valley . . 96
   Lady Clough near the summit of the Snake . 97

THE DERWENT VALLEY 98
   Crook Hill and Ashopton Viaduct from the New
     Reservoir 98
   The Middle Dam in Derwent Dale . . 99
   The dismantled church and Derwent village . 100
   The interior of Derwent Church . . 101
   All that remains of Derwent Hall . . 102
   Looking towards Howden Moor and the Slippery
     Stones from the head of Derwent Dale . 103
   The New Reservoir will ultimately engulf the
     once charming Derwent village . 104, 105

WHARFEDALE 106
   Kilnsey Crag 107
   Ilkley. The Cow and Calf Rocks . . 108
   Bolton Abbey 109
   Bolton Hall 110
   The Wharfe below the Strid . . 111
   The Strid 112
   Kilnsey Crag, Eastern Aspect . . 113
   Kettlewell and Great Whernside . . 114
   Starbotton 115
   Hubberholme Church . . . 116
   Rood Loft in Hubberholme Church . 117

MALHAM 118
   Malham 119
   Malham Cove . . . 120, 121
   The approach to the Cove . . 122
   The river emerging from the base of the cliff . 123

Limestone pavement above Malham Cove . 124
Gordale Scar. The approach . . 125
Limestone cliffs enclosing the Scar . . 126
The two waterfalls in the Scar . . 127

LITTONDALE 128
   Cottages at Arncliffe . . . 128
   The Angler 129
   Hawkswick 130
   The village pump and Arncliffe Green . 131

INGLEBOROUGH 132
   Pecca Falls, Ingleton . . . 133
   Thornton Force 134
   Thornton Beck 135
   Ingleborough from near Ingleton . 136, 137
   Ingleton 138
   June evening on Newby Moor . . 139
   Clapham, Ingleborough Lake . . 140
   Clapham Cave 141
   Gaping Ghyll, looking east . . 142
   Gaping Ghyll, looking west . . 143
   On the verge of Gaping Ghyll Hole . 144
   Penyghent from Selside . . . 145
   The stream runs into Alum Pot through the gap
     in the wall 146
   Alum pot 147
   Penyghent from the verge of Alum pot Hole . 148
   Alum pot from Long Churn, joined by a sub-
     terranean passage . . . 149

PENYGHENT 150
   Ingleborough from Penyghent . . 151
   Penyghent and Horton-in-Ribblesdale . 152, 153
   Penyghent from Horton-in-Ribblesdale Church . 154
   The Beck above Hull Pot . . 155
   Looking into Hull Pot . . . 156
   Hull Pot, looking south . . . 157
   The stream flowing into Hunt Pot . 158
   Penyghent towers above Hunt Pot . 159

DENTDALE 160
   A farm in Dentdale . . . 160
   Sundial Cottage, Dentdale . . 161
   The strange rocky bed of the River Dee . 162
   Road and river run side by side in Upper Dentdale 163
   Dent town from the north-east . . 164
   The cobbled main street of Dent town . 165

CONTENTS—*continued*

WENSLEYDALE 166
   Aysgarth. Lower Fall 167
   Aysgarth. Force 168, 169
   Aysgarth. Middle Fall 170
   The village green at West Burton . . 171
   The village green at Bainbridge . . 172
   Gayle near Hawes 173
   Hardraw Force 174
   The view from behind the Fall . . 175

BUTTERTUBS 176
   The last steep bend in the Pass . . 176
   The largest pot-hole 177
   Swaledale from the cairn on the summit of
    Buttertubs 178
   Buttertubs from the crest of the Pass . 179
   One of the smaller "Tubs" . . . 180
   Two cyclists on the way to Hawes . . 181

KIRKBY STEPHEN 182
   Kirkby Stephen 182
   Kirkby Stephen from the hills to the south . 183

The Cross Fell—Mickle Fell Group seen from a
  low hill to the south of Kirkby Stephen . 184, 185

THE TEES 186
   The rocky bed of the Tees above Winch Bridge . 187
   The Tees at Piercebridge . . . 188
   Cottages at Piercebridge Green . . 189
   The Tees at Barnard Castle . . . 190
   Winch Bridge 191
   High Force. A dull and rainy day . . 192
   Looking downstream from High Force . 193

CROSS FELL 194
   High Cup Nick. The Needle . . 195
   Looking west down the Nick . . . 196
   Looking east to the head of the Nick . 197
   Dufton Green 198
   Cross Fell looms dimly to the north of Dufton . 199
   Cross Fell from Kirkby Thore . 200, 201
   Temple Sowerby Manor . . . 202
   Early shoppers at Appleby . . . 203
   Janet's Foss, Malham 204

Introduction

The Pennines are generally known as the " Backbone of England." The title gives a certain amount of secret satisfaction to those residing in the north, although the southerner might well cavil at it because the lowest vertebra of the backbone only makes its appearance just to the north of Derby. The Weaver Hills mark its commencement and, rising from the Midland plain, are patterned with variegated fields, dotted with prosperous-looking farms, and embellished here and there with fine groups of trees which often crown the rounded summits of these gently swelling hills. To the north the contours of this long mountain range rise gradually to Kinder Scout, and are intersected by many narrow and beautiful valleys which are so well hidden as to be unseen from most of the hilltops in the district. This constitutes the southern section of the Backbone, and as a conglomeration of hills and dales differs much from its northern section, which not only includes the Backbone itself, but also many prominent " ribs." These occur as broad sweeping ridges which themselves enclose on the east the heads of some of Yorkshire's most delightful dales. On the west there are no clearly defined " ribs " directly connected with the main chain, but two of its outliers stand as sentinels which frown upon Lancashire: Pendle Hill dominating Clitheroe, and Bowland Forest overlooking the county town itself.

The most southerly part of the Pennines covers much of Derbyshire, although it does, in fact, encroach upon the very edges of Staffordshire, Cheshire, Yorkshire and even a minute strip of Lancashire. It is familiarly known as the Peak District, though its moors and edges, which are dominated by the flat top of Kinder Scout, scarcely merit the title. On the north of this fine walking country a great industrial belt envelops the shallowest part of the Backbone to join Lancashire with Yorkshire in a welter of factory chimneys. Fortunately these thin out in the vicinity of Wharfedale, and beyond Ilkley the lovely undulating hills, often capped by rounded summits, mark the continuation of the range. This country is typical of the moors at their best and is occasionally distinguished by outcrops of rock on its highest contours, but its great charm lies in its glorious woods, sometimes canopying the roads, but more frequently fringing the rivers, all of which variegate the colouring of the wide sweeping dales.

As a whole this section forms a contrasting prelude to the Craven country which as a wide band of limestone straddles the Pennines and affords a remarkable transformation of the scene and its topography. The softer hues of the moors are here replaced by the whitish tones of the extensive limestone pavements which penetrate the sparse grass to gleam in the sunlight. This part of the country is also characterised by some of the most striking scenery in the whole range, for such well-known show places as Malham Cove and Gordale Scar are found here tucked away from the eye of the casual tourist but well worth the time needed to discover them. Moreover, this region is dominated by Ingleborough and Penyghent, two prominent and shapely mountains whose summits are conspicuous objects in the long skyline revealed to advantage from the distant Lakeland Fells. Nor is this all, for the limestone is riddled with pot-holes whose cavernous recesses carry the mountain streams underground and provide the Speleologist with endless material for geological research.

To the north of this belt the rising peaty moorlands again become prominent and stretch away through vast solitudes which in places are so remote as to be reminiscent of the distant Cairngorms. The contours fall slightly about Bowes Moor, but beyond it the ground swells up again in a great lonely plateau to culminate in Cross Fell, the highest peak in the Pennines and situated in the north-east corner of Cumberland. The delectable valley of the Tees penetrates these hills on the east and is one of the choicest scenic assets of the County of Durham, but to the north they sink down gradually to merge ultimately with the desolate lowlands of Scotland.

The Hills

From the brief foregoing description the reader may well ask how the Pennine country compares with the other mountainous districts of Britain. Generally speaking the chief glory of the Pennines is in the broad sweeping lines of its moors and hills, and while it has a special attractiveness of its own, there is no doubt that it does not display the splendour of English Lakeland, the wild grandeur of the Scottish Highlands, the fretted skyline or soaring Gothic spires of the Coolins, or that sombre barren landscape which is characteristic of Snowdonia. Nor does it possess those spectacular ridges which are the delight of the mountaineer, such as Striding Edge on Helvellyn, Aonach Eagach above Glencoe, or the famous Horseshoe of North Wales. There are, however, many modest but shapely hills, and here Penyghent scores over the rest of the Pennine giants with its southern escarpment disclosing some fine outcrops of gritstone which impart great character to the mountain. There may be some who will dispute its pre-eminence and prefer to give the palm to Ingleborough, but aside from its striking aspect when seen from Chapel-le-Dale, Ingleborough's top appears as a mere hump on a high sprawling plateau. In the same way the proximity of the adjacent high moorland detracts from the impressiveness of Cross Fell, which is the highest hill in the whole chain. Mickle Fell, further to the south, suffers from similar disadvantages, as does Great Whernside also, the massive hill above Kettlewell in Wharfedale. It is strange that this Yorkshire giant should have a more important title than its namesake further to the west, but this is probably due to its bulk alone, because the latter is over 100 feet higher and decidedly more shapely. Baugh Fell and Wild Boar Fell have a fine appearance from the vicinity of Garsdale Junction, and when the mist swirls round Nine Standards Rigg, it too can assume almost dramatic proportions from the low hills above Kirkby Stephen.

The hills of the Peak District are perhaps less striking because the whole area is fairly high, but Lose Hill and Win Hill have a singular charm when seen from certain angles, while the most impressive aspect of Kinder Scout is from the west when the great semicircle of gritstone precipices enclosing the Downfall look gigantic from the low hills above Hayfield reservoir. The southern section is, however, characterised by many fine gritstone Edges, like the long broken battlements of an old fortress, that are unique in our British scenery. They perhaps look their best in the setting sun, when their innumerable splintered facets reflect the evening glow and sparkle like rows of jewels strung across the high landscape. The best of them lie to the east of the Peak, and Stanage Edge is probably the most beautiful of them all. Here the high moorland plateau suddenly ends and a line of supporting precipitous gritstone cliffs, up to 100 feet high, separates it from the first declivities of the valley which sink down gently to the woods fringing the river that threads its floor. To revel in the walk along this Edge you should traverse its full length northwards in the evening while the sun goes down in a blaze of glory; you will then indeed have experienced one of the major delights of the whole district. Gritstone is a joy to the climber and most of the Edges have been fully explored by devotees of this sport. To appreciate the grip this stone can give your feet, you should climb up to Robin Hood's Cave. There is nothing else like it. Stanage Edge is, however, only one of the venues of these sportsmen, for every gritstone outcrop in the Peak is well marked by the boot nails of its enthusiasts. They are widely distributed throughout the district and several of them are noticed in this book. The favourites are probably Cromford Rocks, Cratcliff Tor, Robin Hood's Stride and Kinder Scout in Derbyshire, and Hen Cloud and the Roaches in Staffordshire. While the layer of gritstone on Penyghent is perhaps more striking in appearance, it is more shattered and seems to offer no continuous courses for the climber.

Those who love moorland walking will find the Pennines much to their taste. It is true enough that in Derbyshire most of the moors are inaccessible because they are preserved for grouse, but in spite of the innumerable notice boards warning off the trespasser, people do roam about them as I did to secure the photographs for this book. Some of the moors are protected by fences which approximate in height to the deer fences of the Highlands, and it would be a ticklish job to cross those enclosing Bamford Edge, a fine gritstone escarpment frowning upon the new Derwent reservoir far below. The northern section of the Pennines, however, does not appear to suffer from

10

these disadvantages and those who wish to seek solitude in the high places will find it easily on the Mickle Fell–Cross Fell group of hills. Here the moorland stretches as far as the eye can see and you have to keep a wary glance for the bogs which abound everywhere. It is a good pull to attain the highest part of this great ridge, let lone to walk its full length. You may see a few sheep, but your companions will be the wind and cloud, the plover and the curlew. The peak-bagger will have a happy time in the Pennines because there are so many summits, and, unlike the Lakeland Fells, they are separated by great distances. The views from them are spacious and often repaying; one of the best is obtained from Ingleborough, where to the west you look to the serrated outline of the blue Lakeland hills, and to the east to the seamed façade of Penyghent.

The Craven country is famous for its topography, for aside from such spectacular features as Malham Cove, Gordale Scar and Kilnsey Crag, the whole of this limestone belt is riddled with pot-holes. These are dangerous places in which to loiter, especially on a misty day, but are nevertheless well worth seeing, even from the adjacent moorland, Gaping Ghyll is the most notorious, and it requires a steady head to stand on the verge of the hole and to look down on to the blue haze which camouflages its fearsome depth. Alum Pot is more charmingly situated, for it is surrounded by trees, but the gash itself is awesome, and when you look down and your eyes get accustomed to the gloom you will be able to pick out the ferns which grow in profusion on its sheer walls. All the pot-holes have been explored and here the Speleologist is in his element. He may

descend the main shaft in a Bosun's Chair, or climb down on a swaying rope ladder. This is, however, only an introduction to the game, for he then follows the subterranean passages and chambers, swimming through deep pools of water or fording underground rivers, to delight in the fantastic encrustations, stalactites and stalagmites, all of which glitter faintly in the light of his torch. In addition to these adventurous attractions, there are the beautiful caves near Ingleton and Castleton, most of which can be explored with a guide on payment of a small fee.

A glance at any of the maps covering the Pennines will reveal the wealth of tarns and lakes sprinkled about this long line of hills. Of the small ones, the Mermaid's Pool in the very shadow of Kinder Scout is one of the most charming; when seen from the Edge above, it glitters like a brilliant sapphire on the sombre slopes of this vast peak. Of the larger ones, Semmer Water and Malham Tarn occupy the premier positions, but the barrenness of the adjacent moorland detracts considerably from their appeal and they do not compare favourably with the exquisite lakes and larger tarns of English Lakeland or with the superb and colourful lochs of Scotland. A large number of the sheets of water in the Backbone of England are in fact reservoirs, but it must be admitted that the various bodies responsible for their construction have in many cases done their best to improve the new landscape by planting trees to soften the prospect. Good examples of this planning are the two completed reservoirs in the Derwent valley where the trees have matured sufficiently to make the walk along its winding banks a real pleasure.

AXE EDGE

The Dales

It is in its valleys that the Pennine country is seen at its best. They are not gloomy and impressive like Wasdale or Glencoe, but for sheer beauty are indeed hard to beat. Some of them are narrow defiles, hidden away from the searching gaze of the climber on his hilltop, while others are on the grand scale and wind their way deeply into the fastnesses of the hills. They act as gigantic catchment areas and the rivers which grace them are without compare. There are also an abundance of waterfalls, with a cascade at almost every bend in the stream, so that when you walk along their banks you have water music all the way. What can be more enchanting?

Dovedale is pre-eminent among the sinuous narrow defiles of the district. It is hemmed in by striking limestone pinnacles which rise above the masses of beautiful trees and look down upon the placid stream which the trout fisherman proclaims as his Utopia. Chee Dale, also in Derbyshire, is on a more dramatic scale, but the trains which rush in and out of the tunnels throughout its entire length rather spoil the majestic beauty it once possessed. It is, however, well worth a visit and should be traversed from west to east on a summer evening if its amazing limestone topography is to be seen at its best.

Wharfedale is the loveliest of the larger valleys. It is the pride of Yorkshire and who will dispute it? Here you find a lovely river, fringed with noble trees and graced with delightful villages, passing through a sweeping dale crowned with moorlands, and all within reach of some of our greatest cities. But if you prefer waterfalls and the tinkling music of leaping cascades, go to Wensleydale, where you will find them in abundance. Aysgarth Force is famous and strangely enough most tourists are content to merely see the upper fall from the bridge, whereas the middle and lower forces are infinitely superior, but are seen only by those who care to walk through the woods and descend to the rocky bed of the river. Hardraw Force near Hawes is unique and easily accessible, although you must pass through the parlour of a small inn to see it in comfort. If you love beautiful rivers, you will one day discover the Lathkill, for it is the most placid and peaceful stream I know, especially the stretch of it below Over Haddon, where you may sit on its green mossy banks and see the trout rising to its surface while the gentle plash of water passing over the weirs makes music like the muted strings of a celestial orchestra.

The villages of the Pennines are another great attribute. There is something about them which appeals strongly to romantic folk, for they undoubtedly have a charm and beauty which is difficult to excel elsewhere in Britain. There are many who aver that Tissington is the finest of them all, but I cannot agree with this view, although I subscribed to it before I had seen some of the others. Take Arncliffe, with its sunny village green and overhanging heights—the gem of Littondale; or Kettlewell, with its chattering beck and quaint old houses and inns—the pride of Wharfedale; or Bainbridge, with its spacious green and shady trees—the delight of Wensleydale: all shining jewels in grand and luxuriant valleys. But even these are surpassed by West Burton, a model of dainty architecture tucked away in the folds of the hills off Wensleydale. It is the epitome of peace, quietness and contentment. Here you may relax and laze away the hours amid ideal surroundings, playing a game of cricket with the laughing children of the village or loitering on the smooth turf of the green to chat quietly with the older inhabitants. If you doubt these lofty tributes, look at the pictures in these pages and then go and see the places for yourself. You will perhaps find the village of your dreams to which you will want to retire from the turmoil of the city.

ASKRIGG IN WENSLEYDALE

The Pennine Way

The foregoing notes, together with the monographs which follow, will clearly show those who are unfamiliar with the Pennines that they not only afford an attractive touring ground for the motorist, but also country abounding in beautiful and interesting places, many of which can be seen only by those who are prepared to walk off the beaten track on a journey of discovery.

It is also well known that much of the moorland in the Derbyshire Peak is private ground: the notice boards which acquaint the pedestrian with this unfortunate fact are legion and confront him at almost every turn in the high ground. Further to the north movement is less restricted; nevertheless, something needs to be done so that lovers of the hills and open spaces may have access to them within reasonable limits.

Some years ago the first serious attempt was made to remove these restrictions. In 1888 Mr. James Bryce, who afterwards became Lord Bryce, introduced an Access to Mountains Bill in the House of Commons, but for one reason or another it never reached the Statute Book. This measure proposed that " no owner or occupier of uncultivated mountain or moorland shall be able to exclude any person from walking or being on such land for the purposes of recreation or scientific or artistic study or to molest him in so walking or being." In 1938 Mr. A. Creech Jones introduced a similar Bill and an amended draft of it was submitted to the Ramblers' Association for their approval. So many complications, however, were introduced that when it reached the Statute Book in 1939 this body felt bound to disclaim all responsibility for it. So far no attempt has been made to apply the Act.

Doubtless there are many who will argue that if people want to walk for their health and enjoyment they should stick to the hundreds of miles of roads throughout the country or else be satisfied with the alluring downland paths and mountain tracks which already exist. The first argument is unsound because no real pleasure can be obtained from long road walks owing to motor traffic; moreover such a course completely rules out solitude, a much-prized attribute searched for and treasured by all mountain walkers. The second argument would not arise in either Lakeland or Snowdonia, where every facility is provided for access to the hills, but in the Pennines the paths are few and far between and cover but a small portion of the high ground.

Anyone who doubts this state of affairs should try to amble on Kinderscout, a bare peaty plateau of some thirteen square miles which is uncrossed by a single right of way. He will be lucky if he is not accosted by a keeper and turned back off the moor. That the necessity for legislation is pressing will then be evident, but if still further proof is required he should have attended the annual demonstration in the Winnats near Castleton, where thousands of ramblers used to meet to demand the freedom of the hills.

As long ago as 1935 the desirability of altering these conditions was given further practical shape by Mr. Tom Stephenson, who originated the scheme for a Pennine Way and in the following years advocated it vigorously in the daily Press. The idea was to open a continuous footpath over the high ground from Edale in Derbyshire, along the Pennines, and across the Cheviots to Wooler in Northumberland. The suggestion aroused widespread interest and the Ramblers' Association decided that it merited close examination.

In 1938 the Pennine Way Association was founded at a conference of representatives of the Ramblers' Association, Youth Hostels Association Regional Groups, Footpath Preservation Societies, the Co-operative Holidays Association, the Holiday Fellowship, the Workers' Travel Association and other open-air organisations. The conference unanimously agreed that a Pennine Way was desirable in the national interest, on the grounds of the spiritual and physical well-being of the youth of Britain. It was also agreed that " the wide, health-giving moorlands and high places of solitude, the features of natural beauty, and the places of historic interest along the Pennine Way give this route a special character and attractiveness which should be available for all time as a national heritage of the youth of the country and of all who feel the call of the hills and the lonely places."

The proposed 250-mile route forming the Pennine Way begins at the head of Edale and crosses Kinderscout to the Snake Inn, which is situated in the Woodlands Valley. From there it follows a Roman road and then turns up Alport Dale and over the lonely wilds of Bleaklow to Longdendale. Steering between the industrial blackspots, it meanders across the Saddleworth Moors and on by Standedge, Blackstone Edge and Stoodley Pike to the Calder Valley near Todmorden. Thence it climbs over the moors to the Brontë country, passing the derelict Withens Farm, the supposed original of *Wuthering Heights*, and descending to Ponden Hall. Over another range of moors it continues to Ickornshaw, the birthplace of Philip Snowden, and thence by Lothersdale to the Aire Gap near Skipton. Airedale is followed to Malham and then the way goes by the grim portals of Gordale, over Fountains Fell and Penyghent and down to the Pot-hole country at Horton-in-Ribblesdale. Hawes, in Wensleydale, is reached by way of Ling Gill and an old packhorse road. Across the valley from Hawes is the village of Hardraw, with its fine waterfall, and from there the route climbs Great Shunner Fell on the way to Keld, in Upper Swaledale, and on to Tan Hill, the highest inn in England. Stainmore Gap is crossed *en route* for Middleton-in-Teesdale, and from there the Tees is followed, on the Yorkshire bank, by High Force to Cauldron Snout. Thence the way runs westwards by the lonely farm of Birkdale, and up the valley of Maize Beck through one of the most desolate reaches of the Pennines. From High Cup Nick, on the abrupt western escarpment, a descent is made to the hamlet of Dufton. Cross Fell, the culminating point of the Pennines, is climbed on the way to Garrigill and Alston in South Tynedale, whence the Maiden Way leads to the Roman Wall near Gilsland. Hadrian's ancient frontier is followed to the interesting ruins at Housesteads, and the Way then continues across the moors to the North Tyne at Bellingham, and on to High Rochester in Redesdale. Northwards the Roman road, Dere Street, leads to the camps at Chew Green at the head of Coquetdale, and finally the route follows the Border line as far as Windy Gale and then goes over Cheviot and down to Wooler in Northumberland.

It will be noticed that this track is not the shortest or most direct one between Edale and the Cheviot, the reason being that while keeping mainly to the high ground, it goes to right or left to take in places of scenic or historic interest, and is moreover designed, especially in the northern section, to connect up to best advantage the various localities where accommodation can be found. Furthermore, the route is planned to utilise existing rights of way, and as a continuous footpath it would completely eliminate the necessity of using the metalled roads. Since the formation of the Pennine Way Association local voluntary workers have surveyed the route and the data they have collected are at the disposal of any authority interested in furthering the scheme. It appears that about 180 miles of footpaths already exist out of the total distance of 250 miles covered by the route, so that some 70 miles are necessary to complete it. Only 16 of these are on ground on which rambling has not been restricted, but changes of ownership or other circumstances might interfere with this freedom; 70 miles of new footpaths must therefore be secured to complete the scheme. This would involve the construction of a few rustic bridges across moorland streams, some wooden ladder stiles to avoid damaging the easily deranged dry stone walls, an occasional inconspicuous signpost where the way is not clear, and a cairned route throughout. The latter is the ideal method of marking the footpath because the cairns would be built of local stone and therefore mingle unobtrusively with the landscape.

The realisation of this admirable scheme would be a worthy tribute to those of our fighting men who love the hills, the lonely places, and the many beauty spots of our Island Heritage.

LITTONDALE

DUFTON

Ilam and District

Visitors to the southern part of the Peak District will enter it from Ashbourne, to which there is convenient road and rail access from Derby. Walkers and cyclists bound for Ilam will find the hill leading out of the town to be one of the steepest in the district, but if they travel by train to Fenny Bentley a few miles of strenuous work will be avoided.

Ilam is delightfully situated in the Manifold Valley, its trim and charming little Gothic cottages making a pleasing picture near the Cross and bridge over the river. It is surrounded by hills and those on the south are well wooded and dominated by a conspicuous group of trees known as Hazelton Clump. The northern aspect, however, is more bleak and Bunster Hill marks the beginning of the long barrier separating it from Dovedale.

The village is a good centre for hikers, who are fortunate in having such splendid accommodation at Ilam Hall, an Elizabethan mansion of the last century, and almost hidden from the eyes of the ordinary tourist by the vast semicircle of trees which cloak the hillside. The lovely grounds are interesting because the subterranean stretches of the Manifold River reappear in them and the bubbling waters issuing from the limestone may be seen by descending to the narrow valley which winds its way behind the Hall. A leafy path here leads northwards and crosses the almost dry bed of the river by a swaying suspension bridge. Beyond, it meanders over the open grassy fields, and as one tops the first rise, the broad sweeping bends of the Manifold Valley appear ahead.

I have walked up this valley several times, and while it has not the striking character of the adjacent Dovedale, it nevertheless affords a pleasant excursion. For the first mile or two the path keeps high on the south side of the Manifold Valley until it reaches Throwley Old Hall, now in ruins, and once the seat of the Meverells. Passing through the farmstead beyond, it enters a copse on the skyline and then winds its way downhill towards the 200-feet limestone façade of Beeston Tor. This can be reached by the stepping stones crossing the river at its base, and if desired the small cave of St. Bertram may be entered. The entrance is very narrow and years ago pottery and animal remains were found there. The River Hamps comes in on the left in rainy weather to join the Manifold nearby, and here the path merges with the now disused track of the Old Manifold Railway. At one time this toy line connected Hulme End with Waterhouses: the original stations are still in existence and provide a strange spectacle in this lonely and deserted valley. The path winds in and out of its many folds with the rugged escarpments of Wetton Hill rising steeply on the right. It shortly enters a wooded ravine from which the peaked limestone eminence enclosing Thor's Cave may be observed high above the trees. The circular entrance in the rock face is not seen until the footbridge over the river is reached. This may be crossed, when a sharp pull up the hillside gives access to the track leading into it.

Thor's Cave is one of the sights of the district and should on no account be missed, although the scene as a whole is best viewed from the outskirts of Wetton village, when the amazing gash is backed by the graceful spire of Grindon church on the distant skyline. The cave possesses several remarkable features: the arch is symmetrical, 23 feet wide and 30 feet high, with the floor 250 feet above the bed of the river; human remains have not only been discovered in it, but many relics also. They are now in Derby museum and suggest that the cave was at one time occupied by Celts, Romans and Anglo-Saxons; it is effectively illuminated to a considerable depth by a second narrow and lofty opening on the right, opposite which rises a massive column supporting the arches penetrating still further into the grim recesses of the hillside. Moreover, the proportions are magnificent and the entrance commands an extensive prospect over the hills to the north.

The Weaver Hills lie well to the south of Ilam but may be easily explored by those possessing either a cycle or a car. They are gently swelling eminences and hide many a charming farmstead and village, of which Stanton itself is not the least beautiful. Their extensive verdant slopes are in striking contrast to the rather featureless uplands further to the east and disclose many lovely prospects of the Churnet valley to the south.

Tissington is probably the most beautiful village in this part of the Pennines and the walk to it from Ilam is delightful and repaying. It lies on the east of the Buxton–Ashbourne road and is approached through an avenue of lofty trees. The rustic setting is idyllic: there are neat and trim cottages with gardens ablaze with flowers, an open village green below the Norman tower of a church half hidden by foliage, five wells which never run dry, and Tissington Hall, a Gothic mansion, the seat of the FitzHerberts, which possesses a gate of exquisite proportions.

THE MANIFOLD VALLEY FROM ABOVE THOR'S CAVE

ILAM

BRIDGE OVER THE MANIFOLD AT ILAM

THE WEAVER HILLS FROM STANTON

20

TISSINGTON

21

THOR'S CAVE

MASSIVE COLUMN SUPPORTING THE ARCHES OF THOR'S CAVE

AN ENCHANTING STRETCH OF DOVEDALE
AND THEN DROPS DOWN

24

THE PATH ON THE RIGHT ASCENDS TO THE LOVER'S LEAP
TO TISSINGTON SPIRES

The Dove

The Dove, like the Manifold, rises on the southern flank of Axe Edge, and although the two streams follow an almost parallel course to their junction at Ilam, the former has attained greater fame, not only in literature by the pens of Izaak Walton and Charles Cotton, but also by reason of its more romantic setting, particularly in that section of it between Hartington and Ilam. The river is 56 miles long and is finally received by the Trent at Newton Solney. Throughout the greater part of its course its valley is lovely and varied, in some places pastoral, and in others so spectacular as to give it an unequalled place in the river scenery of England. The most dramatic section is from Milldale to Thorpe Cloud, where the colour contrasts in the spring and autumn between the limestone bastions, the trees, and the stream itself are so exquisitely beautiful as to make it a painter's Paradise and a photographer's Arcadia. Moreover, the river is the dream of the trout fisherman, and those who are able to stay at the Izaak Walton Hotel will soon learn something of the intricacies and disappointments of this fascinating sport.

All those who have descended the steep hill from Thorpe to Ilam will have noticed the little shapely conical hill which stands like a sentinel on the right of the road. This eminence hides the narrow sinuous ravine of the Dove which is best reached by turning to the right over the bridge at the bottom of the hill. Here the scene is pastoral, with cows and sheep grazing in the fields on either side, and the stream making quiet but sweet music as it cascades over the moss-grown weirs beside the road. The prospect changes in the shadow of Thorpe Cloud, but the steep enclosing scree slopes are a mere prelude to the dainty picture which presents itself once the stepping stones have been crossed and the left bank of the stream attained. Here the path from Peveril of the Peak comes in on the right through Lin Dale and the walker passes a stile to continue his ambulations on a stretch of greensward like the soft plush of a Chinese carpet. The track keeps close to the banks of the stream and follows a north-westerly direction, with limestone pinnacles rising above the ash, alder, hawthorn, hazel, and a multitude of other trees, shrubs, heather and wild flowers. After passing the Castle Rocks and the Twelve Apostles on the left, it rises to Sharplow Point, which discloses a beautiful vista of the dale with Tissington Spires rising to a height of some 500 feet on the right. The path drops down under a leafy canopy to pass below these jagged limestone pinnacles, beyond which the great arch leading to Reynard's Cave appears high up on the right. Northwards the defile becomes narrower and narrower until there is only room for the stream to pass between the precipitous cliffs which hem it in. This part is appropriately called the Straits and it leads to the Lion's Head, an impending rock on the right. Here innumerable trees, decked with winding creepers, encroach on the track, while overhead the sombre yews cling tenaciously to the chinks in the face of the towering crags. A little further on the contorted spires of Pickerington Tor rise into the sky on the right, while across the stream and facing them on the Staffordshire side, Ilam Rock overhangs like the spire of a shattered cathedral. A wooden footbridge now crosses the stream to give access to a refreshment hut and to the path through Hurt Wood which mounts to a remarkable viewpoint and one worth attaining. A pleasant meadow opens out ahead and is graced by larches and backed by Raven's Tor, a craggy eminence frowning upon Dove Holes which are reached by a bend to the right. The dramatic scenery of Dovedale is now replaced by less romantic surroundings, and the path meanders on by the stream, to cross it by the pack-horse bridge near the hamlet of Milldale. For a short distance the scene is prosaic and the road is followed to Lode Mill, where a track leads off to the left beyond the bridge to enter Wolfscote Dale. This encloses a very beautiful section of the Dove and the sweeping grassy slopes of the valley are enlivened here and there by outcrops of gleaming limestone. Cows and sheep again make their appearance, but the quiet charm of the scene remains until the dale ends at a bridge where an undecipherable guidepost directs the uninitiated wanderer to nowhere.

Keeping the river on the left, the walker crosses an open field to another footbridge which spans the stream at the entrance to the sylvan glade of Beresford Dale. Here the cliffs mount sharply to the skyline and overhang the laurel and rhododendron which grace the greensward by the river. The way next leads to Pike Pool, where a sharp-pointed crag rises like a stake from the stygian depths of the Dove. It is crossed again by another footbridge, and then the enchanting dale ends abruptly, giving place to open pastures on both sides through which the path meanders until the cottages of Hartington bring one back to the mundane things of life.

DOVEDALE. CASTLE ROCKS

DOVEDALE. STEPPING STONES

28

LOOKING NORTH ALONG DOVEDALE.   TISSINGTON SPIRES ON THE RIGHT

PACKHORSE BRIDGE AT MILLDALE

LODE MILL AND DOVE COTTAGE AT THE ENTRANCE TO WOLFSCOTE DALE

LIMESTONE BASTIONS OF WOLFSCOTE DALE

A QUIET STRETCH OF THE DOVE IN WOLFSCOTE DALE

THE END OF WOLFSCOTE DALE

THE ENTRANCE TO BERESFORD DALE

PIKE POOL, BERESFORD DALE

Matlock and District

One of my earliest recollections is of the annual departure of my father and mother for their holiday in Matlock. I well remember their drive down to the station with baggage carefully labelled, and how they returned in due course rejuvenated by the invigorating hydropathic treatment they had received there. They often spoke of the beauties of the district, and enthused over the charming folk who appeared to revel in the cold water treatment.

A good many years elapsed before I was able to visit the Matlocks, and although I did not indulge in the treatment, I was anxious to see for myself the glories of these towns which had been so much eulogised by my parents. I arrived one autumn evening when the weather was favourable and the first thing that impressed me was the soft light of the setting sun which cast a rosy glow upon the walls of Riber Castle high above the town. Next day I strolled from Matlock Bank through the narrow dale to Cromford, where houses and cottages jostle with one another for a place on the steep sides of the valley and are frowned upon by the towering cliffs of High Tor some 380 feet above the sweeping Derwent which flows by the side of the road. The situation is certainly charming, and while it is fortunate that the scree-slopes below the overhanging cliffs are canopied by a varied array of trees, it is nevertheless a pity that the railway pops in and out of tunnels throughout its entire length, for this detracts considerably from its romantic setting. I was, however, especially attracted by the well-wooded Heights of Abraham facing High Tor, and in the afternoon ascended the zigzag path which climbs up the hill behind the cottages. It soon leaves them behind and after passing through some trees leads ultimately to the Victoria Prospect Tower, which discloses a remarkably spacious panorama of the country surrounding the town. The apparent majesty of High Tor is dwarfed and from here sinks into comparative insignificance, its real relationship with the surrounding hills being revealed with Riber Castle still commanding the extensive prospect.

The Via Gellia is one of the much-praised venues of the district, and one afternoon I rode to the head of the valley enclosing it and walked back to Cromford beneath its leafy decorations, passing the well-situated mill at its junction with the Bonsall road. I shall not easily forget the subtle hues of the trees on this glowing autumn day, for they provided a most colourful picture of arboreal beauty.

This part of the Peak has a fascination for the gritstone climber because a number of outcrops of this rock are accessible to him. The nearest and most easily reached are the Black Rocks at Cromford. They are conspicuous on the skyline after passing the Scarthin Gap in the southward journey out of Matlock and present a grim appearance, with their long overhanging masses of gritstone which point towards the town like the cannon of some commanding fortress. I spent a most enjoyable morning scrambling about the amazing buttresses and gullies of this Cyclopean edifice and found the almost level platform above them to be a superlative coign of vantage for the appraisal of the panorama stretching from east to west. Matlock Bath was conspicuous far below to the north, with the winding course of the Derwent clearly revealed, while the houses of Middleton on the skyline to the west stood out clearly in the morning sunshine. The designation of these rocks is particularly appropriate, for while they are scarcely black in texture, they always appear so as one approaches them because they stand silhouetted against the sky.

Cratcliff Tor is another striking outcrop, but it is more distant and better reached from Great Rowsley. It rises above the trees on the western side of the Winster road, overlooks a rustic farmstead, contains a Hermit's cell and two fine 100-feet buttresses which enclose the Owl Gully, one of the standard climbs in the district.

Robin Hood's Stride, sometimes called Mock Beggars Hall, stands a little to the west of Cratcliff Tor and can be seen above the trees in the walk up to the latter. A path connects the two outcrops and the scramble up to the base of the two isolated pinnacles forming the Stride is well worth the effort. To climbers they are known respectively as the Inaccessible and the Weazle, and their capstones are also fluted like those of the adjacent Tor. They stand roughly 30 feet apart, so that Robin Hood must have been a veritable giant to have stepped across the gap between them. The view to the west is extensive and clearly reveals the rolling uplands of the Peak. A path crosses the fields in a north-westerly direction behind the Stride and gives access to the lane running downhill to Alport, and so to the enchanting Lathkill. On the right of it, and a few hundred yards short of the lane, stands one of the many remarkable stone circles which are found in the Stanton Moor district. There are only four stones on their beam-ends in this one, although it was formerly known as Nine Stones.

A COTTAGE NEAR STANTON-IN-PEAK

MATLOCK. RIBER CASTLE AND HIGH TOR FROM THE HEIGHTS OF ABRAHAM

THE MILL IN VIA GELLIA

41

CROMFORD, LOOKING TO MIDDLETON FROM THE BLACK ROCKS

STONE CIRCLE NEAR ROBIN HOOD'S STRIDE

ROBIN HOOD'S STRIDE

44

CRATCLIFF TOR. THE OWL GULLY

The Lathkill to Earl Sterndale

Those who have discovered the Lathkill, which emerges from a hole in the limestone near Monyash and flows through a valley of sylvan splendour to fall into the River Bradford at Alport, will agree with me that it is one of Nature's most peaceful and captivating creations. The walk from one end to the other calls for no special exertion; in fact you may stroll through the fields which border its lower reaches and saunter along the path beside it for the rest of the way, to loiter at every turn in its course and admire such softness of scene and mellowness of colouring as is difficult to find elsewhere in Britain.

You first cross the bridge which spans it at Alport, where there is a succession of exquisite weirs, and turning to the right through the adjacent farmstead, wander along the path by its banks with the woods rising above the stream on your right. You soon come to Conksbury bridge, with its low arches—a charming little piece of architecture toning perfectly with the surroundings. You cross it and the scene changes. A woodland path keeps close to the stream on the left, and on emerging from the leafy canopy you walk on soft spongy turf as you follow the graceful curves of the river. On either side the colourful slopes of the glen reach up to the skyline, while ahead you perceive the houses of Over Haddon standing above a break in the trees. You pass some cottages on the right below this village and the scene changes again, for the bed of

the river is almost dry as you meander beside it through a wood. Here the trees are so thick that you can scarcely see the sky, and the only sounds to break the silence are the mystic murmurs of the forest. You escape from the trees and the scene changes yet again. You can now see well ahead along the ravine which encloses the trickling stream, and outcrops of limestone appear here and there on the hillside to gleam in the sunshine. You go in and out of the numerous bends, and as you advance the hills become lower and lower until Cales Dale comes in on the left. You pass it and when the next twist is encountered you find the source of the Lathkill in a hole in the limestone wall on the left, but it will be dry unless you are very lucky! The dale narrows and is strewn with boulders, through which you thread your way to come out eventually into the open fields near Monyash. On looking back, you marvel how these rolling hills so effectively hide this inimitable creation of Nature.

If you wish to see the miniature peaks of the district you will take the road from Monyash to Crowdecote. As you descend the steep hill above the village, they confront you at the end of the valley. If you turn to the right at the bottom, the narrow road will bring you to Earl Sterndale, which possesses an inn whose fame has spread far and wide. For the " Quiet Woman " is unique, and you may there quench your thirst in ominous silence!

CHROME HILL FROM CROWDECOTE

RIVER BRADFORD NEAR HADDON HALL

THE LATHKILL AT ALPORT

OVER HADDON AND THE LATHKILL FROM CONKSBURY BRIDGE

LATHKILL DALE AT ITS JUNCTION WITH CALES DALE

The Wye

The River Wye rises in the dim caverns of Poole's Hole at Buxton, and after following a devious artificial course through the town, threads a succession of narrow limestone dales which are famed for their loveliness. It leaves behind these striking scenes below Monsal Dale, and flowing through peaceful pastoral country to Bakewell, continues as a pure limpid stream by way of the open meadows about Haddon Hall, to be finally received by the Derwent at Rowsley.

Thousands of travellers who have gone by rail from Derby to Buxton or Manchester will have glanced out of the carriage windows and seen its glittering surface as the train sped in and out of the numerous tunnels which penetrate the entire length of Monsal, Miller's and Chee Dales. Those with a taste for beautiful valley scenery will have been intrigued by these scanty glimpses, and at the first opportunity will have tramped the three dales from end to end as the only way of discovering their hidden charms. For this purpose they will have stayed in either Bakewell or Buxton and used the bus services between the two towns as a convenient approach to the entrance to Monsal Dale at one end, or to Topley Pike at the other.

Imagine you are going to take this delightful walk on a warm sunny day in late spring, when the trees are dressed in their leafy best, and wild flowers deck the hedgerows. You will have the Wye on your right as you leave Bakewell, but until you reach Ashford-on-the-water it will be too far away for you to notice its intimate details. At this lovely village it flows beside the road, where you will be immediately attracted by the beautiful bridge which has been the subject of many painters and photographers during past decades. The road winds in and out of the gradually narrowing dale with the pine trees forming Great Shacklow Wood on the hillside to the left. In a couple of miles Monsal Dale opens out on the right, and you will take the path with the stream on your right as it skirts the steep slopes of Fin Cop. As you wander through this sylvan paradise you will doubtless notice the sparkling artificial cascade which is almost hidden by the trees on your right. After passing it you will come to the great viaduct which carries the railway across the dale, emerging from Longstone tunnel on the right, and running into Monsal Dale station a little further along the valley to the left. If you have the time and energy you will walk up to Monsal Head to get a more comprehensive view of the dale as it bends sharply to the north-west and in the

far distance discloses the entrance to Miller's Dale. To reach this section of the valley you will cross a bridge and follow the narrow road until it comes to a mill, through which you may walk on payment of a small fee to charity. This gives access to the wide graceful bends of Miller's Dale, which is hemmed in by limestone crags on the left and by overhanging sylvan heights on the right. You will follow its sinuous course and pass another mill to gain the road which winds along by the river, past fine precipitous bastions on the right, until the great steel viaduct carrying Miller's Dale station appears ahead. You will walk below this gigantic structure, and turning sharply to the right beyond it, pass through a gate on the left to enter a sylvan glade which is a mere prelude to the grandest part of Chee Dale further on. As you advance, picking your way over fallen trees and through twining creepers, the trains roar overhead, but you soon leave this pandemonium behind and follow the grassy path which makes a wide circuit round the northern flank of Chee Tor. It bifurcates at the point where the Wye takes a sharp turn to the south, the left branch keeping down by the stream, and the right fork taking a risky course high up along the side of the hill. You will choose wisely by taking the former route, because it is not only the easier path, but also reveals the grand limestone precipices of Chee Tor to far greater advantage. You will soon contact the railway again, and crossing the stream by a footbridge below one of its many tunnels, recross it again to meander along the narrow track by its very edge through a gorge which in places is only just wide enough to admit of its passage, let alone that of the track which is carried by stepping stones below an overhanging crag. The most spectacular section of Chee Dale lies hereabouts on your left where buttresses and pinnacles of white limestone tower into the sky and vie with one another to attract your admiring glances. You will pass in and out of railway arches until you come to some cottages situated below the entrance to Great Rocks Dale on your right, but you cross the footbridge opposite them, and following the rising track through a copse, emerge on the high road at Topley Pike, the sentinel marking the end of Chee Dale.

If you ascend the road on the left in the direction of Taddington, you may scan the rolling walled uplands to the north and see no sign of the hidden dales you have traversed, which form but a mere crack in this vast area of limestone.

WATERFALL IN MONSAL DALE

BAKEWELL BRIDGE

MONSAL DALE

THE WESTERN END OF CHEE DALE
DOWN TO

56

THROUGH WHICH THE WYE FLOWS
MILLER'S DALE

MILL AT THE ENTRANCE TO MILLER'S DALE

MILLER'S DALE

LIMESTONE CLIFFS IN MILLER'S DALE

CHEE TOR

CHEE DALE

STEPPING STONES IN CHEE DALE, BELOW OVERHANGING CLIFF ON THE LEFT

TOPLEY PIKE

GREAT ROCKS DALE

Buxton and District

Buxton is the highest town in the Pennines and stands at an elevation of over 1,000 feet above sea level. Its climate is dry and bracing, but it owes its popularity to the healing properties of its waters rather than to its situation as a tourist centre. The visitors who patronise it, and especially the ladies who stay at the larger and more expensive hotels, are a model of fashionable elegance, as may be seen at any of the concerts and entertainments which are frequently given in the Pavilion, a prominent glass structure in the Gardens. These cover some 23 acres and are one of the principal attractions of the town. They are threaded by the infant Wye which tumbles over several artificial cascades before disappearing into the tunnel which conveys it to Ashwood Dale. There are a number of fine buildings in Buxton, but the most important of them is the Crescent, built over a century ago in the same style as those in Bath.

The Baths are a special feature and much used as a curative agent in cases of rheumatism and like affections. The water supplied to them issues from thermal springs in the limestone at a constant temperature of 82° F., and there is a steady flow of about half a million gallons a day. One of the most interesting places in the town is Poole's Cavern which penetrates Grinlow Hill to a depth of nearly half a mile, but when it is compared with the caves in Castleton, or with those of unrivalled magnificence at Cheddar, it comes a long way behind them for the beauty and variety of its incrustations.

The Goyt Valley provides one of the most delightful excursions in the district, especially that section of it between Goyt Bridge and the source of its river in the northern flank of Axe Edge. A good walker can do the whole round easily in a day, and this section of the valley is best seen by going first to Goyt Bridge and then proceeding upstream. To reach this point it is desirable to follow the Stockport road for about two miles to where it bends round to the right at the top of Long Hill. A rough road here goes off to the left and soon drops steeply downhill with views of the valley spread out below. Goyt Bridge is some two miles from this road junction. The scenery is far removed from that usually associated with the Peak, and is more reminiscent of Westmorland Lakeland, with stooks of rock strewn about the grassy flanks of the hillsides and trees here and there to variegate the prospect. A track runs up beside the Goyt River, and keeping it on the left, passes through sunlit trees for a considerable distance before emerging upon the open moorland. The stream flows down through a narrow ravine and is crossed where the first tributary comes in on the left at Raven's Low. A path follows it to its source and then continues to mount over the moor, until on topping the rise and skirting a wood, it joins the old road descending to Burbage, seen below to the north-east. A walk of about 2 miles brings the pedestrian back into the centre of Buxton. Those who wish to make an alternative exit from the valley may do so by following the old cart track and turning to the right on the moor for the Cat and Fiddle, an inn of renown standing on one of the most bleak and exposed pieces of high ground in the whole district.

Axe Edge is a well-known landmark to the south-west of Buxton. Its highest point is 1,807 feet above sea level, and the Leek road which traverses its eastern flank rises to a height of no less than 1,601 feet. It is thus a hard pull for the cyclist, with free-wheeling compensations in the reverse direction, but the views from it are disappointing and do not compare with those from similar eminences in the district. The windy ride over this elevated causeway is, however, interesting, and there are glimpses of the shapely little peaks around Chrome Hill away to the east.

Ramshaw Rocks form a conspicuous uplift in the landscape some miles to the south, and are seen on the skyline long before they are reached. They are of gritstone and worthy of close inspection, a few minutes only being required to walk up to them across the intervening moor. The most prominent crag overhangs slightly and is shaped like a giant toad when viewed from the ridge further to the south.

A steep hill runs down to the charming hamlet of Upper Hulme, which is situated in a bend of the road leading to the right off the highway. This road swings round to the north-west, and on topping a rise ahead reveals the fine eminence of Hen Cloud, which is garnished with a magnificent outcrop of gritstone, on whose buttresses and gullies the climber sports himself high above the surrounding country.

Beyond it, and further to the north-west, rises the long line of gritstone familiarly known as the Staffordshire Roaches, which vie in popularity with their neighbour as a climbing ground for the expert in this branch of gymnastics. The road below these excrescences becomes rougher and rougher, and at Roach End passes round to the right behind them, ultimately to rejoin the Buxton-Leek highway in the vicinity of the Royal Cottage Inn.

CLIMBERS ON HEN CLOUD. · NO. 1 LEADS THE GRITSTONE BUTTRESS ON THE RIGHT

BUXTON.   THE RIVER WYE PASSING THROUGH THE GARDENS

SUNLIGHT IN THE GOYT VALLEY

RAMSHAW ROCKS

THE TOAD. RAMSHAW ROCKS

71

HEN CLOUD FROM UPPER HULME

HEN CLOUD

73

THE STAFFORDSHIRE ROACHES FROM HEN CLOUD.' NO. 2 IS HALF-WAY UP THE BUTTRESS NOW

HEN CLOUD. NO. 3 FINISHES THE CLIMB

Stanage Edge to the "Surprise"

The Peak District is bounded on the east by a long succession of gritstone Edges which stretch in an almost unbroken line from Mickleden Edge, near Langsett in the north, to Fallinge Edge, overlooking Great Rowsley in the south. They do not in themselves attain any great height, as their precipitous faces seldom exceed 100 feet, but they extend across the horizon at heights varying from 1,000 feet to 2,000 feet above sea level, if Ashop Edge on Kinder is included among them. In general they have a south-western aspect and are thus seen at their best in the afternoon or evening, when the sun imparts a strange luminosity to their splintered facets. There are wide differences in their character and setting, and they vary from the striking isolated tors which rise from the lonely moor as Derwent Edge, to the shattered rocky bastions which stand amid sylvan surroundings as Froggatt Edge. They are all backed by bleak and desolate expanses of moorland, given up largely to grouse, and look down on valleys which in some places are extremely remote and in others populated with farmsteads and charming villages from which they may be easily explored. The subjects of this monograph lie midway in this long line and belong to the latter class. They overlook the Hope Valley and are within easy reach of Hathersage and Bamford, while Sheffield is only a few miles behind them to the east.

Stanage Edge is perhaps the longest line of continuous gritstone in the whole district, and stretches in a north-westerly direction from the highest point on the Hathersage–Ringinglow road, to Stanage End within sight of Moscar Lodge on the Sheffield–Glossop highway. There is a variation of about 100 feet only in altitude throughout its entire length, but its culminating point is at High Neb, which lies well to the north of its centre.

I have explored this Edge in both directions, and while I prefer the walk northwards in the afternoon, as I have already said elsewhere, I shall describe it here in the reverse direction to conform with the arrangement of the photographs accompanying this monograph.

I left the charming village of Hathersage one delightful October morning, when the sun rose over the hills as a red fiery ball and the sky to the south was heavily laden with cloud. There was a pleasant nip in the opalescent atmosphere as I ascended the low ridge which rises between this village and Bamford. As I gained height I perceived the grim bastions of Kinder Scout lying huddled together beyond the graceful outline of Win Hill on the other side of the Derwent Valley, while on my right the cows and sheep grazed lazily in the fields and the conspicuous spire of Hathersage church stood out clearly above the smoky canopy which enveloped the village. The lane mounts gently, first disclosing Bamford Edge, and then the southern escarpment of Stanage, but it was only on approaching Dennis Knoll that I saw the commanding outline of High Neb to the north across the spacious moorland. At this point the lane joins the old cart road which runs from Bamford to Redmires and I followed it to the right for some distance before taking to the open moor, whose dying bracken was just assuming the russet browns of autumn. The walk up to High Neb was pleasant enough and the top of its buttresses easily attained by a nice scramble, so that I was soon standing on the summit of this dominating landmark and scanning the wide panorama which was perhaps most extensive to the south. A track runs along the edge of these little precipices for its entire length of about four miles, and I turned my steps southwards to enjoy this airy and invigorating walk. The cart track already referred to crosses the Edge at its most broken face and a little further to the south Jacob's Ladder surmounts it to provide a short cut to Stanage Pole, a prominent landmark to the east. I passed Robin Hood's Cave and in due course came to the end of the edge at the Cowper Stone, where I found a miscellaneous collection of millstones lying in the heather and bracken and made possibly a century ago, when they were a necessary part of milling machinery.

I descended to the road, and followed it to Millstone Edge, which was brilliantly illuminated by the afternoon sun and stretching across the skyline like an impregnable wall.

The Sheffield–Hathersage road penetrates this massive barrier at Millstone Edge Nick, and on the journey westwards has become famous for its " Surprise View," because after traversing the bleak expanses of Burbage Moor, the sudden revelation of the landscape on a favourable day arrests the attention of the traveller so forcibly that he is bound to pull up to admire it. The verdant slopes of the Hope Valley lie at his feet and stretch away to the west, where they are backed by the serrated skyline extending from Kinder Scout and Lose Hill on the left, to Win Hill, Bamford Edge and to Stanage Edge on the extreme right. The road drops downhill in graceful sweeps through this enchanting dale until Hathersage is encountered at its base.

STANAGE EDGE. HIGH NEB FROM JACOB'S LADDER

HIGH NEB

MILLSTONES AT STANAGE EDGE

MILLSTONE EDGE

WIN HILL AND BAMFORD MOOR FROM THE " SURPRISE "

The Castleton District

Castleton is a good centre from which to explore the scenes described in this monograph. It is situated at the head of Hope Dale, a broad and pastoral valley which unhappily bears the scars of its industrial exploitation. The quaint houses of the village stand in the very shadow of Peveril Castle, which is a prominent object in any view of the dale and easily attained by a zigzag path on the north side. It is, however, unassailable from all others, and its walls actually stand on the edge of the great gash in the hillside which encloses the entrance to the Peak Cavern, while on the south it overlooks the narrow ravine of Cave Dale.

Castleton is famous for its four caves. The Peak Cavern is close to the village, in fact a walk of a few minutes from the Square leads to its impressive entrance. This is so large that until a few years ago ropes were made in the vast semicircular opening at the base of the sheer cliffs which rise overhead for some 300 feet. It exhibits several remarkable features, of which the Eight Arches spanning the subterranean stream some $\frac{1}{2}$ mile from the entrance are by far the most striking.

A walk of $\frac{3}{4}$ mile from the village brings the wayfarer to the Speedwell Mine, which is situated at the entrance to the Winnats Pass. It is one of the wonders of the Pennines, and the boat trip along the straight tunnel, driven into the side of the hill by lead miners over a century ago, is one of the most eerie journeys that can be experienced anywhere in the country. Some $\frac{1}{2}$ mile from the entrance the Bottomless Pit is reached, and to stand there while the waterfall roars into the black recesses far below is indeed a most awesome sensation.

The Winnats is a narrow, sweeping, pinnacled ravine which was originally formed by the action of water on the soft limestone of the district. In the course of centuries this produced a gigantic cavern with a thin roof which ultimately collapsed on the subsidence of the water. A road threads its entire length, but this is so rough that it is used only by pedestrians taking the shortest route to Sparrowpit or Mam Tor.

A little less than $\frac{1}{2}$ mile along the side of the hill to the north of the Winnats is the entrance to the Treak Cliff Cavern. This is the source of blue-john stone, a rare, beautiful, bluish-purple variety of fluor-spar. The cavern also contains a remarkable collection of stalactites and stalagmites which are the best I have seen apart from those at Cheddar.

Some distance further along the main road, and opposite the shattered façade of Mam Tor, is the entrance to the Blue-John Mine. To view the dark recesses of this gigantic swallow involves the descent of some 160 steps as well as several gradients, and its passage leads ultimately to a vast chamber, some 150 feet high, known as Lord Mulgrave's Dining Room. The most interesting feature, however, is the collection of stalagmites known as the Waterfall, for these include horizontal incrustations as well as vertical ones, the latter being the usual form in which they are found.

The Great Ridge hems in Hope Dale on the north and separates it from the spacious valley of Edale. It is the only ridge of its kind in the Peak and affords one of the easiest and most delectable walks in the whole district. It extends for about 4 miles from east to west and is nowhere higher than 1,750 feet. Lose Hill is the conical sentinel standing at its eastern extremity and commands an extensive prospect which reveals to advantage the long line of gritstone edges behind Win Hill across the verdant floor of the Hope Valley. Rushup Edge is the tremendous whaleback rising at its western end, and together with Kinder Scout encloses the head of Edale. Mam Tor and Back Tor are prominent eminences between the two, the former displaying its shivering, shaly face to the south, and the latter its curious ribs of gritstone to the north.

I have traversed this ridge in both directions on several occasions, and while there is not much to choose between them, I think the route from west to east is preferable because the cairn on Rushup Edge is its culminating point and therefore the best coign of vantage for its general appraisal. This hill may be scaled with facility from either side, but it is best approached from Edale by way of Chapel Gate. The track here tops the rise to pick up the broad path from the west which runs along the entire length of its crest. The easiest way to climb it from Castleton, however, is by way of the Winnats and then across the fields to the road rising to Mam Nick, but such a course involves both the ascent and descent of Rushup Edge, and this is often avoided by pedestrians, who merely climb Mam Tor and complete the traverse at Lose Hill. The most noteworthy prospects from it are across Edale towards Kinder Scout, because they clearly disclose the great cloughs which deeply penetrate the flanks of this mountain. The reverse views across the Hope Valley are extensive, with Peveril Castle and Castleton conspicuous on the far side.

83

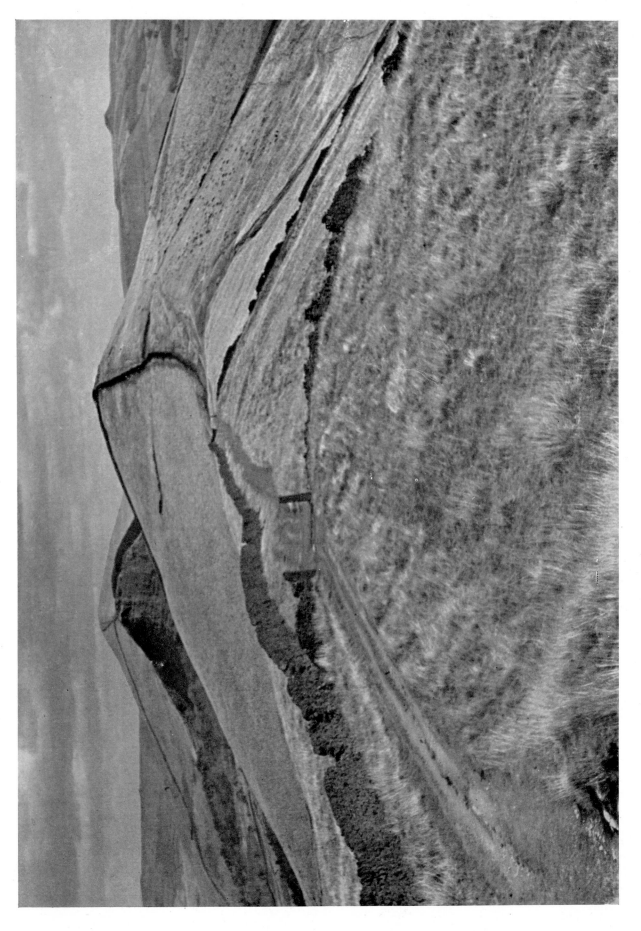

LOSE HILL, BACK TOR AND WIN HILL FROM MAM TOR

BACK TOR

85

MAM TOR, THE " SHIVERING MOUNTAIN "

THE HOPE VALLEY FROM LOSE HILL

EDALE AND KINDER SCOUT FROM THE GREAT RIDGE

RINDSLOW KNOLL IS THE ROCKY POINT ABOVE EDALE

Edale and Kinder Scout

Edale stands on the southern flank of Kinder Scout, about half way along the spacious, pastoral valley of the same name. The village is well known to the mountaineering fraternity as the best centre from which to explore the wild cloughs and vast peaty plateau of Kinder. It possesses a beautiful church whose graceful spire is conspicuous in all the views of it, and two hotels whose proprietor, Mr. F. Heardman, is a climber and cave explorer of no mean order, and who, moreover, is always delighted to place his intimate knowledge of the district at the disposal of his guests. A railway threads the valley and is the connecting link between Sheffield and Manchester, a fact of ominous importance at week-ends when the trains decant hundreds of hikers who quickly disappear in all directions to find healthy exercise on the surrounding hills. A road runs almost parallel with the line, but as there is no exit for it at the dale head, it bends to the south at Barber Booth and passes over to Castleton by way of Mam Nick.

The cottages of Edale are clustered together about the entrance to Grindsbrook, a barren, steep-sided and rugged clough which deeply penetrates the flank of Kinder and is guarded by two lofty heights, Grindslow Knoll on the left, and Ringing Roger on the right. The quaint hamlet of Barber Booth lies a mile to the west, and its neighbour Upper Booth, a similar distance further on, nestles beneath the gigantic exit of Crowden Brook, another superb clough in the Kinder flank. A track continues in a north-westerly direction to Edale Head, mounts the scree of Jacob's Ladder, to lead over the bleak moors to Hayfield. In the opposite direction and facing the narrow entrance to the dale, a further magnificent rift known as Jaggers Clough penetrates less deeply into the eastern flank of Kinder. It is not on the grand scale of the others, but the sylvan character of its lower reaches gives it a special charm of its own.

The circuit of Kinder Scout is an expedition of first importance and its twenty-two miles of varied scenery will appeal to strong walkers who may complete it in a day, but can, if desired, finish their ambulations at Hayfield and return to Edale by bus and train from Chinley Junction. The walk may be undertaken in either direction, but I prefer it from east to west because the vast amphitheatre enclosing Kinder Downfall is best observed by afternoon or evening light. A path leaves Edale by a picturesque pack-horse bridge and crosses the fields to join the road at Nether Booth. A short step beyond this hamlet another path goes off to the left and, mounting the hillside, soon drops down to cross the sparkling stream in Jaggers Clough. It ascends the opposite slopes and rises to the skyline at Hope Cross, where a fork on the right follows the stone wall to Win Hill. Bending round to the left, the main path soon discloses enchanting views of the Woodlands Valley below, and when the descent to this dale is reached, it reveals a delightful vista along Alport Dale, perhaps best known for its Alport Castles, which are the result of a landslide high up on the eastern slopes of the valley. A footbridge carries the path over the Alport River, and on gaining the high road the walker turns to the left along it for the Snake Inn. Those with time to spare may prefer to abandon the highway in favour of the track through Oyster Clough, but although this digression is easier for the feet, its prospects scarcely merit the longer detour. During the walk up the gradually rising road, the views of Kinder on the left increase in grandeur with every step. One of the most magnificent scenes is to the south-west into the rugged confines of Blackden Brook, but it is Seal Edge, and finally Fairbrook Naze, that will hold the gaze of the pedestrian, for they completely dominate the landscape and from this angle assume spectacular proportions. The Snake Inn, well placed among the trees, soon appears on the right, and after taking refreshment here the walker continues ahead for a few yards and then turns to the left through a wall to cross the stream and to enter the wild valley of Ashop Clough.

The path adheres to the left bank of the stream all the way to its source at Ashop Head, and while the walker will delight in its soft music and subtle colouring, he will constantly raise his eyes to the great barrier on the other side of it where the tottering gritstone outcrops of Ashop Edge on the skyline seem to be ready to fall at any moment and overwhelm him. The track goes on and on until it finally peters out in a sea of mud where stakes have been driven in to guide the wayfarer in safety to the col leading over to William Clough. Here the scene changes dramatically, for instead of descending through a barren wilderness, he drops downhill by a trickling stream which threads a ravine clothed in heather, bracken, ferns and trees whose colourful beauty is hard to beat anywhere. Hayfield reservoir appears below and the path descends to its west side, to skirt it, and to pick

(*Continued on page 96.*)

KINDER DOWNFALL

THE HEAD OF EDALE FROM RINGING ROGER

92

CROWDEN TOWER FROM CROWDEN BROOK, KINDER SCOUT

93

MUD GROUGH ON THE SUMMIT OF KINDER SCOUT

FEATHERBED MOSS FROM THE " BOXING GLOVE " STONES ON ASHOP EDGE

WIN HILL FROM WOODLANDS VALLEY. ENGULFING OF OLD ROAD BY NEW RESERVOIR

EDALE AND KINDER SCOUT. (*Continued from page 90.*)

up the track for Edale. The views to the left hereabouts are among the most magnificent in the district and reveal to perfection the gigantic amphitheatre of gritstone about the Downfall, which in hazy weather assumes the grandeur of a wild workshop of the Titans. The track ascends the long crest of one of the Kinder escarpments, and after passing a shooting cabin, undulates over wild moorland until the Hayfield path is joined below Edale Cross. The walk thereafter is downhill only, and when Jacob's Ladder is reached the rough scree may be avoided by taking the grassy path on the right. The hamlets of Upper Booth and Barber Booth follow in quick succession until a field path leads the tired walker back to his hotel in Edale.

The top of Kinder Scout is a vast plateau some 5 miles long and 3 miles wide, intersected in all directions by slippery mud groughs which drain off the water in rainy weather, and scarcely rising above the 2,000 feet contour at any point. It is one of the most sinister mountains I know, and its summit a notoriously dangerous place in bad weather. The most popular ascents from Edale are by way of Grindsbrook or Crowden Brook, but the former is less frequented as it is private and preserved for grouse. The circuit of its Edges affords a splendid excursion providing the walker is not stopped by keepers. With luck he may follow the path all the way round its innumerable indentations and scan with delight the vast landscape which changes with every turn. The most interesting sections are Seal Edge and Ashop Edge, because they are garnished with a miscellaneous collection of strange stones that protrude from the moor and of which the " Boxing Gloves " on the latter are perhaps the most striking. Kinder Downfall is also noteworthy. It is some 100 feet high and in calm, dry weather sports a trickle of water only, whereas after heavy rain, accompanied by a strong south-westerly wind which rushes through the gigantic natural funnel below it like a hurricane, the fall is blown back over its crest and provides one of the most amazing spectacles in the country.

The road familiarly known as the Snake has already been referred to in this monograph. It commences at Ashopton Viaduct and winds its way through the sylvan glades of the Woodlands Valley, climbs the lovely wooded stretches of Lady Clough, and after passing the entrance to Doctor's Gate on the right, traverses the desolate moorland at a height of 1,680 feet, to descend finally in wide curves to the town of Glossop.

LADY CLOUGH NEAR THE SUMMIT OF THE SNAKE

CROOK HILL AND ASHOPTON VIADUCT FROM THE NEW RESERVOIR

The Derwent Valley

The Derwent Valley, so far as it is known to walkers in the Peak, is that section of it which lies between the source of the stream in the remote recesses of Bleaklow and the village of Bamford. Up to a few years ago this dale was occupied by peaceful farmsteads and quiet villages, but its vast catchment area was acquired in 1899 by the Derwent Valley Water Board, who have since completed the construction of two reservoirs where the water is impounded by massive and lofty dams of stone, and are at present finishing the third and lowest one where the huge barrier of earth and stone blocks the valley just to the north of Bamford. This has involved the erection of two tremendous viaducts at Ashopton and Ladybower, together with the dismantling of the charming villages of Ashopton and Derwent. The former is already under water, which at its final level will be 100 feet above the old village, while the latter is in process of disintegration and the rising lake is at present lapping the steps of the lovely church and its adjacent cottages. Sad as this may be, it is not all, for the beautiful centuries-old Derwent Hall, for years the home of one of the most delightfully situated Youth Hostels in Britain, has also been pulled down and parts of it too are already under water.

I did not know this valley before its metamorphosis, so that when I visited it I was unable to draw any comparisons between its natural and changed aspects. I do, however, like the glint of water in the landscape and I love trees, so that in consequence I found the upper part of the valley enchanting and reminiscent of a Scottish glen with its conifers coming right down to the water's edge, and especially in the vicinity of Slippery Stones. This prospect was therefore reassuring after the sad sight of the shattered Derwent village and I can only hope that in years to come the new reservoir will assume an equally attractive appearance.

The Derwent Valley thus affords an appropriate exit from the Peak to the northern section of the Pennines, and beyond Slippery Stones the wayfarer ascends the moorland slopes to pass Margery Hill on the right, to traverse the dreary wastes of Cut Gate, and to descend to Langsett and Penistone. Here he will find transport to take him through the industrial blackspots and to set him down again, in Ilkley perhaps, where he may continue his fascinating exploration of our homely hills and dales.

THE MIDDLE DAM IN DERWENT DALE

THE DISMANTLED CHURCH AND DERWENT VILLAGE

THE INTERIOR OF DERWENT CHURCH

ALL THAT REMAINS OF DERWENT HALL

102

LOOKING TOWARDS HOWDEN MOOR AND THE SLIPPERY STONES FROM THE HEAD OF DERWENT DALE

THE NEW RESERVOIR WILL ULTIMATELY ENGULF

THE ONCE CHARMING DERWENT VILLAGE

Wharfedale

Wharfedale lies in the bosom of the Pennines, and as a spacious curving valley it stretches northwards from the very threshold of some of our great industrial cities to peter out in the distant fastnesses of the hills about Oughtershaw. The lower section as far as Threshfield and Grassington is richly wooded and flecked with historic buildings, whereas the trees thin out higher up, limestone crags appear, and beyond Kettlewell the hills close in until it finally merges with the desolate moors which separate it from Ribblesdale. No wonder the Yorkshire folk are proud of it, but there are thousands of others who come from the four corners of our country to pay homage to it, to steep themselves in its charms, and to return to their homes with glowing memories not only of its placid beauty but also of the kindly dalefolk who people its captivating villages. Wharfedale is in truth the epitome of tranquillity.

Those who are fortunate enough to live in the adjacent towns can get a general idea of this valley in a day's motor journey, but like tourists who merely pass through it, they miss much of its intimate atmosphere by not staying in one or other of its delightful villages which are dotted about throughout its entire length. The lower reaches of the dale are well seen on foot from Bolton Abbey, Burnsall or Grassington, while the more remote corners can be explored from Kettlewell or Buckden.

Everyone has heard of Ilkley Moor, which rises to the south of the town of Hydros. It provides fine walking country, and its prominent outcrop of gritstone known as the Cow and Calf Rocks, which overhang Ben Rhydding, are the resort of the climber and scrambler. Moreover, these rocks form a splendid viewpoint and reveal to advantage the dale and surrounding hills where the famous Blubberhouses Moor stretches across the skyline to block the prospect to the north.

A few miles away Bolton Abbey stands on the west bank of the Wharfe and is overlooked by a tree-clad escarpment whose rocky base acts as a breakwater in the sharp bend of the wide river. The ruins are surrounded by groups of noble ash and are beautifully placed amid the luxuriantly wooded valley and closely enclosing hills. Part of them is transitional Norman; the nave, which is perfect, is Early English and Decorated; the transepts and choir are in ruins. Bolton Hall rises just behind the Abbey and is a building of splendid proportions: the manor is held by the Dukes of Devonshire. The road threading the dale passes along the side of the extensive park and the Hole in the Wall is a well-known break in its enclosure. The Strid is situated about two miles upstream in Bolton Woods, and exhibits one of the finest scenes of water play in the district. The rocks in the bed of the valley form a narrow channel through which the stream rushes and gurgles, while the myriad leaves of the surrounding trees reflect the sunlight and impart a strange beauty to the prospect. The gorge appears to be so narrow that an athlete might easily leap across it, but should he slip and fall into the torrent he would probably lose his life.

Proceeding northwards along Wharfedale, the traveller will soon espy the massive ruin of Barden Tower, and on climbing the hill beyond it will note the conspicuous rocks of Simon Seat high up on the right across the river and frowning upon the little village of Appletreewick far below. The subsequent run down discloses Burnsall, with its beautiful bridge at the bottom of the hill, and on leaving behind its quaint cottages Threshfield and Grassington are soon encountered.

The road rises gently with many undulations and bends as it enters Upper Wharfedale, and after passing the village of Conistone, on the east bank of the river, it approaches the overhanging bulge of Kilnsey Crag. This spectacular limestone cliff, which on closer inspection proves to be more massive than its first appearance suggests, is of great geological interest as the eastern extremity of the gigantic belt of limestone which characterises the Craven country.

A short distance beyond it Littondale opens out on the left, and after crossing the River Skirfare by a pretty bridge, the road then goes up and down along the flank of the hill to cross another bridge into Kettlewell. This delightful village, hidden away in the hills and standing astride a tuneful beck, is affectionately known to thousands of hikers for its quaint cottages and inns.

Continuing now along the east side of the river, we soon encounter Starbotton, with its cottages tucked away below the brow of Cam Head, and then Buckden follows with its houses round the green and overshadowed by Buckden Pike, which just tops the 2,300-feet contour. Here the road bifurcates, the right branch going over the hills to Aysgarth in Wensleydale, and the left fork following the winding course of the Wharfe past Hubberholme and on towards Oughtershaw. Hubberholme church is famous for its Rood Loft which is one of the few surviving examples in England.

KILNSEY CRAG

ILKLEY. THE COW AND CALF ROCKS

BOLTON ABBEY

BOLTON HALL

THE WHARFE BELOW THE STRID

111

THE STRID

KILNSEY CRAG, EASTERN ASPECT

KETTLEWELL AND GREAT WHERNSIDE

STARBOTTON

HUBBERHOLME CHURCH

ROOD LOFT IN HUBBERHOLME CHURCH

Malham

After staying in Wharfedale for a week I left it on a dreary day to cycle from Kettlewell to Malham with two heavily laden rucksacks slung over the back wheel. Those who are familiar with the narrow sinuous road connecting this dale with Airedale can well imagine how I pushed the machine up the steep gradients, hoping to free-wheel down the other side of the hills. But I found the sharp bends too dangerous, and had to walk a good part of the way. However, there were compensations, for I was bound for the Buck Hotel, and here I must pay a tribute to the kindness of the proprietor and his wife, who entertained me there alone for several days although they had arranged to close the place for a week in order to give themselves and their staff a holiday. Mr. Wiggins was at one time a professional photographer and we therefore had much in common to talk about. Among other things we discussed the difficulties of camera work in the adjacent countryside, and I hope readers who are not particularly interested in this hobby will forgive me for here dilating upon the problems involved in taking pictures of Malham Cove and Gordale Scar—the two most spectacular features of the Pennines which have drawn thousands of tourists to gaze in admiration upon their magnificence.

Malham Cove stands in the side of the hill about a mile from the village. According to my altimeter it is over 300 feet high and forms a gigantic semicircle of overhanging limestone cliffs, which owing to the action of water and frost are striated vertically, and at the foot of which the infant Aire emerges as a substantial stream. Three terraces are festooned across the face of the precipices; the lowest one may be easily negotiated by anyone with a steady head, but those above it are broken by a gap in the centre and any attempt to traverse them would meet with disastrous results, because, as every climber knows, limestone is too slippery to admit of firm footholds. Swallows and swifts nest on these terraces and haunt the nearby stream and pastures in search of flies. The whole chasm faces slightly west of south and the essence of the problem of its effective portrayal is not only to convey an accurate idea of its scale and grandeur, but also to capture every detail of its majestic façade.

I had carefully examined all the published photographs I could find, but for one reason or another they were unsatisfactory and merely gave a chalk-and-soot impression of it. It is no good photographing the Cove in bad weather, of which I experienced several days on arrival, but they gave me the opportunity to study its topography so that when the sun shone I should already know the advantageous viewpoints and the best time of day to visit it. I came to the conclusion that between 1 and 2 p.m. G.M.T. would afford the best lighting to reveal all the detail I was anxious to secure, and when conditions ultimately favoured me this proved to be correct. At other times the overhanging upper terrace would cast shadows of such magnitude that the right or left extremities of the face would be obscured. The most dynamic viewpoint I discovered was on a projecting ledge of the upper terrace, but when I climbed up there to take the frontispiece for this book, the wind was so violent that I had to crawl out on to its extremity and, while lying down, hold the camera over the edge of the precipice and hard against it to obtain stability. Altogether I exposed 24 frames, of which those included herein are typical examples and I think give a satisfactory impression of its grandeur. The limestone pavement above the Cove is a revelation and should be inspected by all those who can ascend either of its flanks. Moreover, the dry bed of the stream, which centuries ago plunged over the cliffs, is well worthy of examination providing the wayfarer does not venture too near the edge.

Gordale Scar is situated some one and a half miles to the north-east of Malham and may be reached from Mastiles Lane, which goes over the hills to Kilnsey. Access to it is obtained through the yard of a small farm, but a section of the road may be avoided by crossing the fields lower down and following the stream as far as the pretty fall known locally as Janet's Foss. The approach to the Scar is impressive, but the precipitous scree slopes hide the chasm itself and give no idea of its dynamic appeal until they have almost closed in upon the walker and he suddenly rounds a bend on the right to find himself overwhelmed by their magnificence. On either side of him they tower into the sky like the gigantic walls of a Titan's workshop; the right wall overhangs to a considerable extent and is particularly impressive. A stream gushes out of a square window high up in the limestone face and lower down forms a waterfall whose noise reverberates through this fantastic gorge.

Malham Tarn lies about two miles to the north of the village and is overlooked by Malham Tarn House, but the landscape is bare and comparatively uninteresting and scarcely worth the effort needed to reach it. Malham village itself is charming, with quaint whitewashed cottages and a lovely green.

MALHAM

MALHAM COVE. THE LIMESTONE

LIFFS ARE OVER 300 FEET HIGH

THE APPROACH TO THE COVE

THE RIVER EMERGING FROM THE BASE OF THE CLIFF

LIMESTONE PAVEMENT ABOVE MALHAM COVE

GORDALE SCAR. THE APPROACH

125

LIMESTONE CLIFFS ENCLOSING THE SCAR

THE TWO WATERFALLS IN THE SCAR

COTTAGES AT ARNCLIFFE

Littondale

As I have said elsewhere Littondale branches off from Wharfedale, and following a straight north-westerly direction, passes the villages of Litton and Halton Gill to finally merge with Foxup Moor to the north of Penyghent. The brows of the steep sides of the valley are embellished with scars, its green strath is decked with farmsteads, and the River Skirfare flows peacefully throughout its entire length. Its villages are a delight to the eye and are often tucked away at the foot of the frowning crags, while Arncliffe itself is a perfect picture, complete with a green shagged with trees, a pump, charming cottages and a fine old church. Like many rivers in the Pennines, the Skirfare is sufficiently rich in trout to attract the angler in the season, and he will find in this remote dale that solitude which enables him to ply his rod and line in seclusion.

I had frequent opportunities to chat with these sportsmen when I asked just what induced them to prefer it to one of the more energetic pursuits. Since it may interest others, who like myself know nothing of its fascination, I give here a consensus of their opinions:

1. Angling automatically brings you to the most beautiful surroundings in the country.

2. It allows the intimate observation of wild life, for after 15 minutes the rats and birds approach and take no notice of you.

3. It permits the study of insect life of the river.

4. It requires much knowledge, only acquired by long experience, to tell the position of trout feeding at all heights of the stream throughout the seasons, for it is one of the established facts that the trout will find a position in the stream where he can obtain maximum food supplies with a minimum of labour. Boulders are favourite venues when the fish takes up a position in the eddy. The fisherman's art is to cast his fly into the water in such a manner that it is carried to the feeding fish in the same way as a natural fly, that is, without a drag on the line. It is, moreover, essential that the angler make himself inconspicuous because he is readily spotted by the trout.

THE ANGLER

HAWKSWICK

THE VILLAGE PUMP AND ARNCLIFFE GREEN

Ingleborough

Ingleborough is one of the great landmarks of the Pennines. Rising to a height of 2,373 feet, it dominates the vast moorland triangle based upon Ingleton and Settle. The summit consists of a conspicuous square gritstone cap which is well seen from the heights of Penyghent and Fountains Fell to the east, and from the roads threading the Bowland, Pendle and Brontë country to the south, while it is also a prominent eminence in the Pennines skyline when observed from the distant Lakeland Fells to the west. Its flattish top carries four cairns, of which the highest and largest overlooks the extensive landscape to the south-west, but its chief interest is that as one of the Craven Highlands it stands upon the vast belt of limestone which is riddled with pot-holes, not only on the massif itself, but also on the adjacent hills and dales.

Clapham is conveniently situated for the exploration of this hill country because it lies within easy reach of the reigning peak and is accessible by main road and rail. Moreover, the charming cottages of the village stand astride a beck fringed with trees and it affords an approach of greater variety and interest than any of the others. Ingleborough House is well placed above it and the path runs through its delightful grounds where trees and wild flowers mingle colourfully and provide glimpses of the placid waters of its tree-girt lake. It winds its way uphill through dense woods to the accompaniment of water music provided by Cave Beck, which cascades through a ravine low down on the right. Emerging from its leafy canopy, it enters narrow verdant pastures, and keeping close to the stream, soon passes the entrance to Clapham Cave on the left, which is situated at the base of a massive outcrop of limestone. Just beyond it the stream from the subterranean passages of Gaping Ghyll rushes out from a hole in the limestone and the track goes ahead through a narrowing dale which on turning to the left reveals the imposing ravine of Trow Gill. Centuries ago this probably carried off the water from the eastern flank of Ingleborough, and on first acquaintance seems to afford no exit, but by carefully ascending the loose scree and boulders in its dim recesses, a narrow opening is found which leads out on to the moors. The path follows the stone wall on the left for some distance and then crosses it when the open ground is reached. Here a guide-post discloses Fell Beck in the direction of Ingleborough summit to the north, and a meagre track goes towards it which is the key to the discovery of Gaping Ghyll in a depression in the vast stretches of moorland. This astonishing hole in the ground is three miles from Clapham, and the subsequent climb up to the summit of Ingleborough takes a direct line across the bog until its southern escarpment is reached. A sharp scramble attains this extensive top and the walk along it soon brings the wayfarer to its cairns.

Gaping Ghyll is the finest pot-hole in Britain and may also be reached by way of Clapdale Farm and Raygill plantation. It receives the waters of Fell Beck, whose tributaries have their source on the slopes of Ingleborough and Simon Fell at a height of about 2,100 feet. In two miles it reaches limestone at 1,350 feet and begins to sink in its bed, but the unabsorbed water flows into Gaping Ghyll. The pot-hole is roughly circular in shape and large enough to take a horse and cart without touching its grim, fern-decorated, vertical walls, which are not protected in any way. The shaft is 340 feet deep and at 190 feet there is a notorious ledge, below which the Great Hall opens out. This is the main chamber with a floor space of half an acre and one of the largest in the world. Measuring 479 feet long, 82 feet wide and 110 feet high, it would contain one of our smaller cathedrals. Connected with it is a complex system of passages and deeper pot-holes extending some 3,110 yards underground, which together with the 900 yards of Clapham Cave in the same series, total nearly 2½ miles of caverns. A glance into this yawning chasm should be sufficient to warn off would-be adventurers, though it may be inspected safely by those who do not suffer from vertigo.

Alum Pot is perhaps the next most interesting pot-hole. It lies on the eastern slopes of Simon Fell above the hamlet of Selside. Its ugly mouth is surrounded by trees and protected by a stone wall through which the stream passes to fall in a single plunge of 210 feet. The total depth of the chasm is 295 feet, but the shaft is blocked some distance down by a gigantic boulder known as the " Bridge." Three hundred feet of rope ladders are required for its direct descent, but if the side passage known as Long Churn is used, half this length only is needed.

Ingleton Falls and the nearby White Scar Cavern are the resort of the tourist The former involves a long enchanting walk through the woods and the stream is frequently crossed by foot-bridges near some of its most famous falls, although by far the most beautiful of them, Thornton Force, is on the open moorland above.

PECCA FALLS, INGLETON

THORNTON FORCE

134

THORNTON BECK

INGLEBOROUGH FROM

NEAR INGLETON

INGLETON

138

JUNE EVENING ON NEWBY MOOR

139

CLAPHAM, INGLEBOROUGH LAKE

CLAPHAM CAVE

GAPING GHYLL, LOOKING EAST

GAPING GHYLL, LOOKING WEST

ON THE VERGE OF GAPING GHYLL HOLE, 365 FEET DEEP

PENYGHENT FROM SELSIDE

THE STREAM RUNS INTO ALUM POT THROUGH THE GAP IN THE WALL

ALUM POT. THE HOLE IS IN THE CENTRE OF THE GROUP OF TREES

PENYGHENT FROM THE VERGE OF ALUM POT HOLE

ALUM POT FROM LONG CHURN, JOINED BY A SUBTERRANEAN PASSAGE

Penyghent

I saw Penyghent for the first time in 1912 when I spent a fortnight in Settle. On the first clear day I noticed its brow rising above the intervening moorland about Stainforth, and it so fascinated me that at the earliest opportunity I climbed to its summit. Conditions were then so bad, however, that my chief recollections are of the mist swirling round its cairn to hide the spacious views of the surrounding country. On the present occasion I was more fortunate, and the glorious day with its azure sky, fleeting clouds and limpid atmosphere will linger long in my memory. I had cycled from Clapham by way of Giggleswick Scar, to be welcomed by the kindly folk at the Golden Lion in Horton-in-Ribblesdale. This comfortable hostel stands opposite the fine old church of St. Oswald, above which Penyghent rises in eternal solitude and majesty.

The mountain reaches an altitude of only 2,273 feet, and lies due east of Ingleborough, which stands on the opposite side of Ribblesdale. It overlooks one of the most interesting pot-hole centres in the Craven country and may be easily ascended from Horton across the gentle slopes of the heather-clad moorland. While Penyghent is inferior in height by 100 feet to its western neighbour, it has a bolder and more shapely outline, which is accentuated by the fine layer of gritstone below its summit. A grassy cart track goes up the hillside from the village and in about 1½ miles ends at a small building. Both Hull Pot and Hunt Pot are close to it, and thereafter the open moors lead up to the broad ridge which in the south culminates in the rounded summit of the mountain.

I left my hotel on a sparkling morning in mid June, when the sunlight was so brilliant that the dry stone walls glinted almost blindingly against the sparse grass which covers the approaches to the moor. I was soon breasting the slopes of the hill where the road undulates slightly amid the outcrops of limestone before reaching the building, now apparently used by the local shepherds. Here these men of the hills were tending their lambs while the ewes bleated mournfully outside the gated enclosure. A cheery word, a reminder of the dangers of the pot-holes, and a friendly adieu faded from my ears as I walked forward to Hull Pot, whose vast yawning mouth breaks the depression in the adjacent moor. The cavern is surrounded by a derelict stone wall, doubtless originally built to prevent the sheep from falling into it, but as I approached, an isolated member of the flock was ambling on its very edge, evidently in search of those inaccessible succulent blades of grass which often draw these animals to their doom. The roof of this pot-hole fell in centuries ago and its floor is now fully exposed for all the world to see. It is 60 feet deep, 60 yards long and 20 yards wide. When the beck above it is in spate it tumbles into the gash beside a rowan tree whose blossom and perfume on this occasion attracted me as I passed round the rim of the hole to walk in the direction of the stream. Higher up this shallow valley the water came down from the hills in volume to provide many a lovely cascade, but as it approached the gash it sank into its limestone bed to emerge from a hole in the side of the pot near its eastern end.

I walked over to look into Hunt Pot, which is perhaps 200 yards away in the direction of Penyghent and slightly higher than its neighbour at an altitude of 1,350 feet. Here the surface depression is 60 feet wide, but the gullet proper is only 20 feet long and 6 feet across at its centre. The ends taper and a jammed boulder at its western extremity enabled me to stand above the chasm and to look down into its grim depths where the sides were covered with moss, lichen and ferns in great profusion. The hole has two pitches, the first 100 feet and the second 60 feet, and after getting used to the gloom I could just pick out the stream taking its single plunge down the first one. Again I found a lonely rowan tree here and it struck me as strange that in nearly every instance I had discovered one of them actually growing on the verge of each chasm.

I now turned my steps in the direction of Penyghent, and taking a direct line for a depression in the ridge, was soon striding gaily along its crest. The cairn stands on the south side of a conspicuous stone wall, and when I reached it the whole panorama lay spread out before me like a great coloured map. Ingleborough rose into the sky as the most prominent peak to the west, but I could easily perceive the eminences of Pendle Hill and Bowland Forest away to the south. I followed the stone wall for some distance and then left it to scramble down the southern bastion supporting the summit. Here I found an armchair depression in the towering wall of gritstone and it afforded me a comfortable seat in which to eat my lunch. What a superb viewpoint for such a feast! I revelled in the wide expanse of country spread out at my feet, and in due course traversed the gritstone ledges until they petered out in the hillside. Then I took a bee-line for the pot-holes and gazed into them again before descending to my hotel for tea.

INGLEBOROUGH FROM PENYGHENT

PENYGHENT. THIS GREAT PENNINE HILL RISE

ABOVE HORTON-IN-RIBBLESDALE

PENYGHENT FROM HORTON-IN-RIBBLESDALE CHURCH

THE BECK ABOVE HULL POT

LOOKING INTO HULL POT

HULL POT, LOOKING SOUTH

THE STREAM FLOWING INTO HUNT POT

PENYGHENT TOWERS ABOVE HUNT POT

A FARM IN DENTDALE

Dentdale

Dentdale penetrates the western outposts of the Pennines, and, as a short valley, rises gently from the outskirts of Sedbergh to end in the steep declivities between Whernside and Widdale Fell where the road goes over into Ribblesdale. Here the L.M.S. main line follows a tortuous course through the hills, traversing tunnels and bridges, to keep well up on the breast of the slopes above Dentdale, which is revealed almost in its entirety to the rapt gaze of the passing traveller. The enclosing slopes of this valley are steep and impart a more compact appearance to it than that assumed by some of the wider and more open dales. Rise Hill shuts it in on the north and Middleton Fell, Crag Hill and Whernside enclose it on the south. It is resplendent with farms and cottages, while the town of Dent itself is so delightfully quaint and charming as to resemble the crystallised model from a child's story book.

Dentdale is not so inaccessible as some may suppose, for the railway high above Lea Yeat affords a convenient starting point and its metropolis may be reached in a leisurely walk of under two hours. You leave the elevated platforms of this remote station and descend the rough road which drops sharply downhill to Lea Yeat, a collection of cottages under shady trees which fringe the playful waters of the infant Dee. Here you join the highway, and turning to the right along it, proceed in a westerly direction with the stream on your left. This is worthy of attention because for some distance it runs along a rocky bed where ledges, holes and diminutive pinnacles have been worn and polished by the water. The road winds along with the patterned fields extending well up the hillsides on either hand, and you pass many a dainty cottage with gardens ablaze with flowers. When you reach High Chapel you may look up the wild rift of Deepdale on the left and see the road which comes over the lofty pass from Ingleton. The houses and church tower of Dent Town soon appear ahead, and after crossing the river by a graceful stone bridge, you approach it with the certain knowledge that you will here find something unique among the towns and villages of the Pennines. The road bends to the right and you are soon enclosed by the maze of little cottages and shops, with happy children playing carelessly in its almost deserted streets. After passing the church on the right you come suddenly upon the cobbled Market Place, which is surrounded by some of the most romantic buildings in the country. On the right you will observe the obelisk of Shap granite placed there in memory of Adam Sedgwick, the founder of the modern science of geology. He was born in Dent Vicarage on March 22, 1785, and died on January 22, 1873. The place was once the capital of the Western Yorkshire dales, but that position is now occupied by Sedbergh.

SUNDIAL COTTAGE, DENTDALE

THE STRANGE ROCKY BED OF THE RIVER DEE

ROAD AND RIVER RUN SIDE BY SIDE IN UPPER DENTDALE

163

DENT TOWN FROM THE NORTH-EAST

164

THE COBBLED MAIN STREET OF DENT TOWN

Wensleydale

Wensleydale will always live in my memory for its poetic waterfalls and romantic villages. Considered as general valley scenery it reveals none of the broad wooded sweeps of Wharfedale, none of the wildness of Swaledale, and none of the spectacular limestone features of either Dovedale or Wyedale, but for individual scenes of waterplay, or for charming villages whose cottages are tastefully arranged round village greens, it is without compare.

The best part of the dale lies between Leyburn and the source of its river, the Ure, which rises on the boundary of Westmorland at Ure Head. Here Lunds Fell frowns upon the road and railway which thread the valley to pass through Mallerstang for Kirkby Stephen, and in the reverse direction to branch to the east at the Moorcock Inn and Garsdale Junction respectively to give access to the towns and villages all the way down to Leyburn and the fertile valleys of Yorkshire beyond. The dale runs almost due east-west, excepting near its head where it bends to the north to end at the county boundary at a height of 1,194 feet. It is graced by a number of subsidiary dales, all of which bring their quota of streams to swell the Ure, and by Semmer Water, which is usually considered to be the largest natural lake in Yorkshire. A general conception of Wensleydale may be obtained from either road or railway, but if its hidden nooks and crannies are to be discovered, the car or train must be abandoned and they must be searched for on foot.

Proceeding westwards from Leyburn, the village of Wensley is soon encountered. It is almost internationally famous for its cheese, which is, however, made also by many farmers elsewhere in the dale. Bolton Hall lies some little distance beyond it and is shortly followed by Castle Bolton on the northern slopes of the valley. The Castle itself completely dominates the scene hereabouts; it was built in the fourteenth century and was the home and stronghold of the Scropes. Carperby is the next village on this side of the dale, and opposite it stands Aysgarth, whose church rises above the trees which hem in the river in this enchanting section. The middle and lower Forces cannot be seen from the road, although the upper fall is visible from the bridge across the river. Much of the water is here side-tracked to a mill and it is only worthy of observation in very wet weather, whereas the other two are at all times a delight to the eye and reached by a path through the woods on the north side of the stream. The middle fall has a single plunge of

perhaps 20 or 30 feet, while the lower one passes over a number of ledges picturesquely placed between the trees, and these widen out until the stream becomes a succession of glittering cascades which can be approached by the wayfarer who climbs down on to the rocky bed of the river when the water is low.

At Aysgarth the highway should be deserted in favour of the side road to West Burton, which stands at the entrance to Walden Dale. This exquisite village is so charming with its lovely cottages, quaint shops and inns, which are delightfully placed round a green whose grass might well have originated in Cumberland, and where peace and contentment reign over its 1820 monument and well-preserved ancient stocks. Crossing the river again, Askrigg is soon reached. It is perched on the side of the hill and discloses fine views of this part of the dale. By turning to the left beyond it the wayfarer enters the portals of Bainbridge, another village of enchantment with shady trees and cottages arranged at intervals round its extensive green.

Continuing westwards again, Hawes is soon sighted on the rising ground ahead, and its charm is enhanced by the adjacent villages of Appersett on the one hand and by Gayle on the other; the houses of the latter standing on the edge of the wide stream which cascades beautifully over broad ledges, but which in dry weather are the playground of its children. Hardraw Force lies in a deep cleft in the hills on the northern slopes of Wensleydale and may be seen on payment of a small fee. The entrance is through the parlour of the Green Dragon Inn, and the fall itself, which is part of Fossdale Gill, is one of the most graceful in the country. It plunges in one uninterrupted drop of nearly 100 feet from the rim of limestone which overhangs the receding banks of soft shale. The adventurous wayfarer may walk close behind it and secure an unusual view of the ravine through its myriads of luminous drops of water. The approach, however, is prosaic and lacks the romantic aspect of the upper gorge because a bandstand still stands beside the stream and in the centre of the green.

Wensleydale now becomes wilder and is overlooked by the heights of Great Shunner Fell on the north, and by Widdale Fell on the south. From the Moorcock Inn it has a barren aspect, and on swinging round to the north beneath Baugh Fell, enters perhaps its wildest stretches, which in a few miles end at the Westmorland boundary.

AYSGARTH. LOWER FALL

AYSGARTH FORCE.   THE SPARKLING CASCADES

OF THE LOWER FALL, ONE OF THE FINEST IN BRITAIN

AYSGARTH. MIDDLE FALL

THE VILLAGE GREEN AT WEST BURTON

THE VILLAGE GREEN AT BAINBRIDGE

GAYLE NEAR HAWES

HARDRAW FORCE, 100 FEET HIGH

THE VIEW FROM BEHIND THE FALL

THE LAST STEEP BEND IN THE PASS

Buttertubs

The pass familiarly known as Buttertubs is the connecting link between the upper sections of Wensleydale and Swaledale to the north. It carries a well-metalled road whose gradients are gentle enough to be easily negotiated by the smallest of cars, and after crossing wild expanses of moorland reaches the col between Great Shunner Fell and Lovely Seat at a height of 1,726 feet, to pass the " Tubs," and then to descend into Swaledale. While this form of travel has the advantages of speed and comfort, motorists miss much of the impressiveness of the pass, and since the walk over it from Hawes to Muker and back may be easily accomplished in a day, I followed this course on the present occasion.

The approach on the south lies on the opposite side of the valley from Hawes and is reached by a road from the station which passes the golf course. When I commenced the ascent it was deserted, so that the cloud and wind, together with the call of a curlew, were my only companions. The first rise is fringed with trees, and on leaving them behind there are charming views on the left into Fossdale Gill which rises in the flank of Great Shunner Fell. The flattish summit of this hill dominates the scene all the way to the top of the pass, but the rough moorland slopes of Lovely Seat on the right rise at such an angle that the cairn is invisible all the way. After leaving behind the last cottage of High Shaw, the road ascends more steeply, and as one reaches the open moor, poles driven in the ground act as route indicators in severe winters, when the pass is snowbound. As I wandered along these undulations ewes and their lambs walked across the road and seemed so accustomed to human beings that they took no notice of me. The final rise is gentle enough and reveals the cairn standing on the crest of the pass, a few yards to the left of the road. I climbed up to it to observe the impressive sweep on the other side, where the road falls, to rise again, before finally dropping down into Swaledale.

Those who do not know the significance of the name of this pass might well slip past the " Tubs " in a car with scarcely a glance at them, but those on foot cannot fail to notice these strange and unexpected infant pot-holes, because they are quite different from anything else in the district. There are about half a dozen of them, varying in depth from perhaps 20 to 60 feet. Contrary to the usual smooth walls of these chasms, they have peculiar ribbed sides with similarly striated flat-topped pinnacles, all of which are worn away by water trickling down the soft limestone. They are grouped together beside the road, which runs on the edge of steep scree slopes and is protected by a rather frail wooden fence.

A long rise beyond them brings the wayfarer to a prominent bend in the road which reveals Swaledale far below. A succession of curves follow and these descend to the highway threading the valley, where Muker lies to the right and Keld to the left. Walkers bound for Bowes Moor will take the latter course and on the way pass Tan Hill, which at 1,732 feet claims to possess the highest inn in the country.

THE LARGEST POT HOLE

SWALEDALE FROM THE CAIRN ON THE SUMMIT OF BUTTERTUBS

BUTTERTUBS FROM THE CREST OF THE PASS

ONE OF THE SMALLER " TUBS "

TWO CYCLISTS ON THE WAY TO HAWES

KIRKBY STEPHEN

Kirkby Stephen

After completing my exploration of Wensleydale, I continued my journey northwards by way of Mallerstang to Kirkby Stephen. This quiet little town lies in Westmorland, and my object in going there was to climb to Nine Standards Rigg on the county boundary, and to examine the strange stones which give it the name. The ascent is easy enough by way of the hamlet of Hartley, and at Fell House, a farm situated in the wilds of the moor, the cart track terminates, and a tributary of Birkett Beck is followed over Hartley Fell which is the prelude to this commanding viewpoint. On this occasion, however, I was unlucky, for the mist came down to blot out the wide vista of the Eden Valley to the north-west.

Before I departed next morning the sun shone for a while and I ascended the low hill on the south of Kirkby Stephen to scan the vast panorama to the north where the long line of hills culminating in Cross Fell were revealed in their entirety. Mickle Fell was a prominent eminence dominating the extensive moorland on the right, and the skyline extended northwards beyond the reigning peak to terminate in the blue haze about the Scottish border. I could, however, pick out the shapely cone of Dufton Pike below it on the left, and was later able to examine this landmark more closely when I spent an enjoyable afternoon in the village which nestles beneath it.

KIRKBY STEPHEN FROM THE HILLS TO THE SOUTH

THE CROSS FELL—MICKLE FELL GROUP

EN FROM A LOW HILL TO THE SOUTH OF KIRKBY STEPHEN

The Tees

The River Tees rises on the southern flank of Cross Fell in Cumberland and for a few miles forms the boundary between this county and Westmorland. After it has been joined by Crookburn Beck, its left bank enters the county of Durham, but when Maize Beck flows into it below Cauldron Snout, its right bank passes into Yorkshire, and it remains the dividing line between these two counties for the rest of its course until it enters the North Sea. The river is about 85 miles in length and in the early part of its course passes through some of the wildest country in the Pennines where hills and bleak moorland afford scenes of desolate grandeur. At Cauldron Snout it forms a series of rapids and flows over a bed of hard rock consisting of black basalt. Trees soon appear to soften the barren landscape, and at High Force it provides one of the finest falls in England. Here both evergreens and deciduous trees fringe its banks in profusion, and on entering pastoral country its scenery becomes gentler and more picturesque. At Middleton-in-Teesdale it assumes more stately proportions and then passes the town of Barnard Castle, followed by Eggleston Abbey and Rokeby. At Winston the valley opens out and the broad river meanders across the rich plain below Darlington, to become finally a waterway of great commercial importance where the ports of Stockton-on-Tees, Thornaby-on-Tees and Middlesbrough form an outlet for the iron-workings of Cleveland in the North Riding of Yorkshire.

Teesdale is closely associated with Queen Elizabeth, for she spent much of her girlhood at Streatlam Castle, where her family estates extended for miles on both banks of the river, and included Mickle Fell, 2,584 feet, the highest peak in Yorkshire, together with grouse moors and farmlands. The Castle has been held by one line since the twelfth century, though heiresses have carried it by marriage successively to Trayne, Bowes and Lyon.

During the exploration of this valley I made my headquarters at Middleton-in-Teesdale, and had it not been for the chance of meeting my son, who at that time was in the Army and stationed at Catterick, I should not have seen the lower reaches of the river. As it was, we met in Darlington one day, and preferring the country to the city, we went out to Piercebridge for lunch and to spend the glorious afternoon by the river. This stretch of the Tees is well wooded and possesses much charm; moreover, it seems to appeal to the swimmer, for many of them were enjoying its cool waters on that hot summer day. The village is enchanting, and its lovely cottages stand round a green where shady trees add much to its delight.

Barnard Castle is beautifully situated on the steep northern bank of the Tees. The graceful mediæval bridge spanning the river, and the picturesque old houses adjoining it, are dominated by the grand ruin where the Balliol family were nurtured, and together make an attractive subject for the camera. The castle is the principal scene of Sir Walter Scott's *Rokeby*, and is worth seeing, as is also the Bowes Museum, built in 1892 in the French chateau style. This is reputed to have cost £100,000, and houses a private collection of porcelain, pictures and tapestries. The industry of Barnard Castle was formerly that of carpet making, first in the hand loom and then in the factory, while the tanning of leather and manufacture of shoe thread were also important. The environs are interesting and beautiful, for Eggleston Abbey stands on the Yorkshire bank of the river, and both Streatlam Castle and the massive fourteenth-century Raby Castle lie some little distance to the north-east of the town.

The villages of Lartington, Cotherstone and Ronaldkirk stand on the east of the Tees and are charming, while Middleton-in-Teesdale is a splendid centre not only for its river scenery but also for the walks over its adjacent hills. Winch Bridge lies just off the main road a few miles to the north of the town and is picturesquely placed amid the woods shagging a narrow gorge. Immediately above it the country is more open and the river comes down over a wide stretch of black basalt to form glittering cascades and placid pools in its course. A mile further on High Force is perhaps the river's most spectacular feature, for here it passes between two great bastions of basalt as a magnificent fall, and when in spate forms a second and smaller cascade on the right. It is approached by a delightful winding path which threads a wood of tall conifers, and those who wish to view the force from above may do so by climbing some steps on the right and scrambling over the adjoining rocks. Here the scene upstream is one of desolation backed by high moorland, whereas the view downstream through the gorge is a sylvan prospect of enchanting loveliness.

The wild recesses of the dale beyond are best explored from Langdon Beck, where a Youth Hostel adds to its amenities. The striking ravine of Cauldron Snout should be visited, but it involves a long moorland walk. It is passed by those wayfarers who are bound for Dufton by way of Maize Beck and High Cup Nick.

THE ROCKY BED OF THE TEES ABOVE WINCH BRIDGE

THE TEES AT PIERCEBRIDGE

COTTAGES AT PIERCEBRIDGE GREEN

THE TEES AT BARNARD CASTLE

190

WINCH BRIDGE

HIGH FORCE. A DULL AND RAINY DAY

LOOKING DOWNSTREAM FROM HIGH FORCE

Cross Fell

Cross Fell is the highest peak in the Pennines. Rising to a height of 2,930 feet, it stands just inside the Cumberland border where the county boundary between it and Milburn Forest passes Tees Head, which lies in the col between them. The mountain is really the culminating point in a high moorland plateau, and its summit is an almost indistinguishable heap of stone. Its topography thus differs much from the general aspect of the Cumberland hills, which for stern grandeur are difficult to beat elsewhere in England. Let it not be supposed, however, that this particular group of hills, which terminates in the south at Mickle Fell, is entirely deficient in interest excepting as a mere high-level walk, because its traverse from Langdon Beck by way of Cauldron Snout and High Cup Nick to Dufton provides not only striking scenes of water play and desolate moorland grandeur, but also one of the greatest surprises in the hill country of Britain.

After leaving behind the wild gorge of basalt at Cauldron Snout, you follow Maize Beck by the wire fence which marks the Yorkshire county boundary. Striking due west up the vast expanse of moorland, you keep to the rather indistinct track among the bent, heather and bog until the plateau is attained about the 2,000-feet contour. The gentle slopes of Dufton Fell rise on the right and those of Mickle Fell and Murton Fell on the left, but between them you soon perceive the blue serrated skyline of the Lakeland Fells far away to the west. You descend slightly and then the grand metamorphosis in the landscape is suddenly revealed, for High Cup Nick drops away spectacularly at your feet just as if the Titans had gouged out a wild rift in the hillside. The whole of its sheer semicircular rim is lined with a series of basaltic columns consisting of small buttresses and gullies, with here and there a needle of rock, while the steep slopes below are strewn with scree which varies in size from a tiny pebble to a small cottage. The track goes to the right and skirts the edge of the precipices, and as you advance there are increasingly broad views of the verdant, patterned Vale of Eden far below. When the rock buttresses merge with the slopes of the moor, you follow a line of cairns which bear away to the right and guide you to a deserted quarry. On passing through a gate below it you pick up a grassy cart-track which meanders down the slopes of Peeping Hill and discloses Dufton Pike away to the right as a shapely conical eminence dominating the village of the same name. You pass through gated pastures, with a lonely farmstead on the right, and descend to a lane which leads down to the main road with the village of Dufton on the right.

This is one of the most charming spots hereabouts, and its picturesque cottages, inn and Youth Hostel are pleasantly arranged round an oblong green which is cut by the road diagonally and ornamented by a well-executed stone fountain. Here you will see the flat top of Cross Fell above the houses away to the north, but if you wish to obtain a better view of it, you must go on to Kirkby Thore, which clearly reveals its dominating position in the long line of hills.

In its very shadow stands Temple Sowerby Manor, known formerly as Acorn Bank, and now the home of Mrs. McGrigor Phillips (Dorothy Una Ratcliffe, the well-known authoress). I had the pleasure of meeting this lady some time ago in Patterdale when she asked me to call, and I therefore took the opportunity of doing so on the present tour.

The village is often described as the Queen of Westmorland, a title well merited by its beautiful situation in the Eden Valley, for its old cottages, greens, and Crowdundale Beck all combine to make it attractive. The stately front of the manor, with its weathered red sandstone, framed by noble trees and engirdled in summer by a perfect galaxy of red flowers, is well seen in the northward approach from the village.

Temple Sowerby was originally Sowerby only, but soon after the manor came into the hands of the Knights Templars it became Temple Sowerby, to distinguish it from Brough Sowerby and the other Sowerbys in the north. There appears to be no evidence to show how the manor came into the hands of the Knights Templars; it was theirs in 1228 and probably before that date. It is a charming place, much rebuilt in the eighteenth century, with fragments of a fourteenth-century stronghold. The house has a magnificent oak staircase of Cromwell's day and there are fine buildings round three sides of the courtyard. In front of the east wing is a sun-dial bearing a curious inscription giving a conversation between the Passenger and the Dial.

Since the ancient property was acquired by Mrs. Phillips it has been completely restored and is now a splendid example of period architecture and period decoration. She has gracefully bequeathed the estate to the National Trust, together with a sufficient endowment for its upkeep in its present condition.

Appleby is the county town of Westmorland and a convenient centre for the exploration of the Vale of Eden. It possesses many quaint houses, a castle, a fine church, and the famous Moot Hall which stands in the market square.

HIGH CUP NICK. THE NEEDLE

LOOKING WEST DOWN THE NICK

LOOKING EAST TO THE HEAD OF THE NICK

197

DUFTON GREEN

CROSS FELL LOOMS DIMLY TO THE NORTH OF DUFTON

CROSS FELL

FROM KIRKBY THORE

TEMPLE SOWERBY MANOR

EARLY SHOPPERS AT APPLEBY

JANET'S FOSS, MALHAM

INDEX

Access to Mountains Bill	13
Airedale	14, 118
Alport	38, 46
Castles	90
Dale	13, 90
Alum Pot	11, 132
Appersett	166
Appleby	194
Appletreewick	106
Arncliffe	12, 128
Ashbourne	16
Ashford-on-the-Water	52
Ashop Clough	90
Edge	76, 90, 96
Ashopton Viaduct	96, 98
Ashwood Dale	66
Askrigg	12, 166
Axe Edge	11, 26
Aysgarth	106, 166
Force	12, 166
Back Tor	82
Bainbridge	12, 166
Bakewell	52
Balliol family	186
Bamford	76, 98
Edge	10, 76
Barber Booth	90, 96
Barden Tower	106
Barnard Castle	186
Baugh Fell	10, 166
Beeston Tor	16
Ben Rhydding	106
Beresford Dale	26
Blackden Brook	90
Black Rocks, Cromford	38
Bleaklow	13, 98
Blubberhouses Moor	106
Blue-John Mine	82
Bolton Abbey	106
Hall	106, 166
Woods	106
Bowes	186
Moor	9, 176
Museum	186
Bowland	132
Forest	9, 150
Boxing Glove Stones	96

Bradford River	46
Brontë Country	132
Bryce, Lord	13
Buckden	106
Pike	106
Buck Hotel	118
Bunster Hill	16
Burbage Moor	76
Burnsall	106
Buttertubs	176
Buxton	52, 66
Cales Dale	46
Cam Head	106
Carperby	166
Castle Bolton	166
Castleton	11, 82, 90
Cat and Fiddle	66
Cauldron Snout	14, 186, 194
Cave Beck	132
Dale	82
Chapel Gate	82
Chapel-le-Dale	10
Cheddar	66, 82
Chee Dale	12, 52
Tor	52
Cheviot	13, 14
Chrome Hill	66
Churnet Valley	16
Clapham	132, 150
Cave	132
Cleveland	186
Clitheroe	9
Conistone	106
Conksbury	46
Cotherstone	186
Cotton, Charles	26
Cow and Calf Rocks	106
Cowper Stone	76
Cratcliff Tor	10, 38
Craven Country	9, 11, 106, 132, 150
Cromford Rocks	10, 38
Crookburn Beck	186
Cross Fell	9, 14, 182, 194
Crowdecote	46
Crowden Brook	90, 96
Crowdundale Beck	194
Cut Gate	98

Darlington	186
Deepdale	106
Dennis Knoll	76
Dentdale	160
Dent Town	160
Derby	9
Derwent Edge	76
River	38
Valley	98
Doctor's Gate	96
Dovedale	12, 26
Dove Holes	26
Downfall	10, 90, 96
Dufton	14, 186, 194
Fell	194
Pike	182, 194
Earl Sterndale	46
Edale	82, 90, 96
Eden Valley	182, 194
Eggleston Abbey	186
Fairbrook Naze	90
Fallinge Edge	76
Fell Beck	132
Fin Cop	52
Fishing	128
Fossdale Gill	166, 176
Fountains Fell	14, 132
Foxup Moor	128
Froggat Edge	76
Gaping Ghyll	11, 132
Garsdale	10, 166
Gayle	166
Giggleswick Scar	150
Glossop	96
Gordale Scar	9, 11, 118
Goyt Valley	66
Grassington	106
Great Ridge	82
Rocks Dale	65
Shacklow Wood	52
Shunner Fell	14, 166, 176
Grindon	16
Grindsbrook	90, 96
Grindslow Knoll	90
Grinlow Hill	66
Haddon Hall	52
Halton Gill	128
Hamps, River	16
Hardraw Force	12, 166

Hartington	26
Hartley Fell	182
Hathersage	76
Hawes	14, 166, 176
Hayfield	10, 90
Heardman, F.	90
Heights of Abraham	38
Hen Cloud	10, 66
High Chapel	160
Cup Nick	186, 194
Force	14, 186
Neb	76
Tor	38
Hope Cross	90
Dale	82
Valley	76
Horton-in-Ribblesdale	14, 105
Hubberholme	106
Hull Pot	150
Hulme End	16
Hunt Pot	150
Ilam	16, 26
Rock	26
Ilkley	98
Moor	106
Ingleborough	132, 150
House	132
Ingleton	11, 132
Falls	132
Jacob's Ladder	76, 90
Jaggers Clough	90
Janet's Foss	118, 204
Jones, A. Creech	13
Keld	14, 176
Kettlewell	12, 106
Kilnsey Crag	11, 106
Kinder Downfall	10, 90, 96
Scout	10, 13, 76 82, 90, 96
Kirkby Stephen	166, 182
Thore	194
Ladybower	98
Lady Clough	96
Lakeland Fells	9, 132, 194
Langdon Beck	186, 194
Langsett	76, 98
Lartington	186
Lathkill	12, 38, 46
Lea Yeat	160
Leyburn	166

Limestone Pavements	118
Litton	128
Littondale	12, 106, 128
Lode Mill	26
Long Churn	132
Longstone Tunnel	52
Lose Hill	10, 76, 82
Lovely Seat	176
Lunds Fell	166
Lyon	186
Maize Beck	14, 186, 194
Malham	118
Cove	9, 11, 118
Tarn	11, 118
Mallerstang	166, 182
Mam Tor	82
Manchester	52, 90
Manifold Valley	16, 17
Margery Hill	98
Matlock	38
Mermaid's Pool	11
Mickle Fell	10, 182, 186
Mickleden Edge	76
Middlesbrough	186
Middleton-in-Teesdale	14, 186, 194
Milburn Forest	194
Milldale	26
Miller's Dale	52
Millstone Edge	76
Nick	76
Millstones	76
Monsal Dale	52
Head	52
Monyash	46
Moorcock Inn	166
Moot Hall	194
Moscar Lodge	94
Mud Groughs	96
Muker	190
Murton Fell	176
Nether Booth	90
Newby Moor	139
Newton Solney	26
Nine Standards Rigg	10, 182
Oughtershaw	106
Over Haddon	12, 46
Oyster Clough	90
Peak Cavern	82
Peeping Hill	194
Pendle Hill	150
Penistone	98
Pennine Way	13
Penyghent	10, 14, 128, 132, 150
Peveril Castle	82
Phillips, Mrs. McGrigor	194
Pickerington Tor	26
Piercebridge	186
Pike Pool	26
Poole's Hole	52
Pot-holes	132, 150
Queen Elizabeth	186
Quiet Woman	46
Raby Castle	186
Ramshaw Rocks	66
Ratcliffe, Dorothy Una	194
Raven's Low	66
Tor	26
Redmires	76
Ribblesdale	106, 150, 160
Riber Castle	38
Ringinglow	76
Ringing Roger	90
Roaches	10, 66
Robin Hood's Cave	10, 76
Stride	10, 38
Rokeby	186
Ronaldkirk	186
Rood Loft	106
Rowsley	76
Rushup Edge	82
St. Bertram's Cave	16
Scott, Sir Walter	186
Scropes	166
Seal Edge	90, 96
Sedbergh	160
Sedgwick, Adam	160
Selside	132
Semmer Water	11, 166
Sharplow Point	26
Sheffield	76, 90
Simon Fell	132
Seat	106
Skirfare, River	106, 128
Slippery stones	98
Sparrowpit	82
Speedwell Mine	82
Snake	90, 96
Inn	90
Stainforth	150
Stanage Edge	10, 76

Stanage End	76
Pole	76
Stanton	16
Moor	38
Starbottom	106
Stephenson, Tom	13
Stockton-on-Tees	186
Stone Circles	38
Streatham Castle	186
Strid	106
Surprise View	76
Swaledale	176
Taddington	52
Tan Hill	14, 176
Tees	186
Teesdale	186
Temple Sowerby	194
Manor	194
Thornaby-on-Tees	186
Thornton Force	132
Thorpe	26
Cloud	26
Thor's Cave	16, 17
Threshfield	106
Throwley Old Hall	16
Tissington	12, 16
Spires	26
Topley Pike	52
Trayne	186
Treak Cliff Cavern	82

Trent	26
Trow Gill	132
Upper Booth	90, 96
Hulme	66
Ure Head	166
River	166
Via Gellia	38
Walton, Izaak	26
Waterhouses	16
Weaver Hills	16
Wensley	166
Wensleydale	12, 106, 166, 176
West Burton	12, 166
Wetton Hill	16
Wharfedale	12, 106
Whernside	160
White Scar Cavern	132
Widdale Fell	160, 166
Wiggins, Mr.	118
Wild Boar Fell	10
William Clough	90
Winch Bridge	186
Win Hill	10, 76, 82, 90
Winnats	82
Winston	186
Wolfscote Dale	26
Woodlands Valley	90, 96
Wooler	13, 14
Wye	52, 66

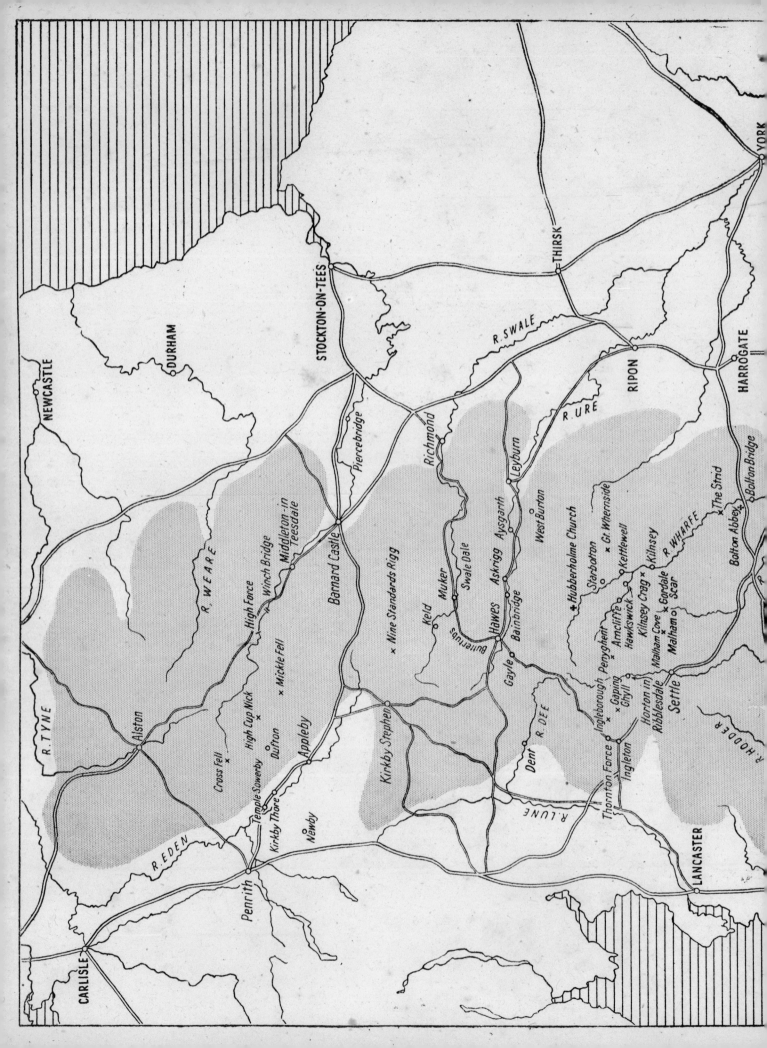